UNDERSTANDING OUR SPIRITUAL GROWTH

A Seven Step Journey to Spiritual Maturity

Dr. Charles Walls, Th.D.

© 2021 by Dr. Charles Walls, Th.D.

ALL RIGHTS RESERVED
No portion of this book may be reproduced in any form without permission from the publisher, except as permitted by U.S. copyright law.

For permissions contact:
twgpllc@gmail.com

Published by
The Walls Girls Publishing Group
P O Box 278
Diboll, TX 75941-0278
www.thewallsgirls.com

ISBN: 978-1-63983-000-8 (eBook)
ISBN: 978-1-63983-100-5 (Soft Cover)
ISBN: 978-1-63983-001-5 (Hard Cover)

PREFACE

No one grows spiritually without knowing what spiritual growth entails. What has been your understanding of spiritual growth? How do you determine it? How do you know if you are growing spiritually? What requirements do you use to measure your spiritual growth? These questions may be a challenge to you but they are critical in knowing what spiritual growth is and how to determine it.

The six days of recreation and the seventh day of rest, when they are deeply studied with the intent of each day teaching us what standards or works we must do, will show us how we are to grow spiritually. The seven steps, represented by the seven days, will clearly show us what is required of us to grow to spiritual maturity.

The insights provided in this book will lead you to discovering a new world where you and your church members will take on a new way of life and see the spiritual growth that will take place within you.

You will be able to discard your old thinking of how to grow spiritually and experience the richness of developing yourself as God would have you do. You will immediately come to know what level of spiritual growth you have attained.

What are the benefits of knowing what the requirements are for growing spiritually? One benefit will be that you will no longer be spending your precious time and energy engaged in church activities, but rather, doing the work of God in leading the unsaved to Christ and ministering to the saved according to their spiritual needs. Let us now take this journey together.

For years, as a Christian, I did not know how to determine my spiritual growth. Like so many others, being spiritual, and developing spiritually, meant having been baptized, going to church, taking part in the activities at the church made available to the members, such as mission, prayer meeting, Bible study, brotherhood, choir, Sunday school, training union, going to association and convention meetings, participating in Bible drills, Easter plays and programs, Christmas speeches, plays, and programs, bake sales, raising money through various type of efforts, and annual programs of the church. If we were blessed to have opportunities to take church sponsored trips to different states and visit historical sites, we felt we were doing the things that would develop us spiritually. Little did I know that spiritual growth was an entirely different experience.

Having gone through undergraduate and graduate seminary, I had not been exposed to learning about how to determine my spiritual growth. Even as a pastor, this subject was spoken of but not taught in any detail that the congregation could use for determining their spiritual growth. One year the Pastor of Sunset Baptist Church, Grand Prairie, Texas, Reverend Matthew McGruder invited me to come to their church and teach in an institute on the subject, "Moving to the next level." God led me to approach this topic from the point of view as steps to our spiritual growth. It was so enriching and motivational to me in developing the lectures on "Moving to the next level."

The intent of this book is to provide the Christian with seven steps or stages of spiritual growth as seen from the six days of recreation and the seventh day of rest, Genesis 1:3- 2:2. Getting to know our spiritual growth level is important because it provides us with the incentive to continue our walk with God daily, and seek those specific elements for growth at each level. We will see the simplistic approach that if followed, will develop us to spiritual maturity.

The aim of this book is to address the need of spiritual growth in the church. The church is problematic, anemic, and stunted; mainly because too many believers, when we meet, only meet to greet, eat, argue, fuss, fight, and return home without ever having a real encounter with the Lord Jesus Christ. This lack of experiencing God leaves believers stunted in spiritual growth. We do not experience God when what we do is mere formality, show, or entertainment, be it in our attempt to worship God, or participate in ministry, or take part in prayer, or engage in praise, or involve ourselves in service. Therefore, the aim of this book is to bring believers face to face with God who will set us before His divine mirror and show us our faults, failures, and sins so we can look to Him for restoration, reconciliation, guidance, and growth.

The Purpose of this presentation is to help us recognize where we are in our spiritual growth; acquaint us with the criteria at each level of the seven levels of spiritual growth; to clarify what is needed to move from where we are to the next level; and to make it known that we must master or meet the requirements of the lesser level before we are able to engage in the works of the next higher level. These levels must be achieved in chronological order.

In addition, this book is to challenge the believer to investigate their spiritual growth to determine what level of growth they have attained. Without this knowledge, the believer will go through the motions of church involvement and church activity believing they are growing spiritually. Understanding our spiritual growth will help us devote ourselves to God and the assignment God gives us.

As part of the purpose, I will endeavor to provide measurable means for believers to assess who they are, where they are in their spiritual growth, and what they must do to continue growing spiritually. It is to aide us in overcoming our unfruitful gathering at the house of God without any rhyme or reason. None of these measurable efforts can become realized without the aid of the Holy Spirit. It is the Holy Spirit who molds us into the image of Christ. Only then will we have any real purpose in life and be able to receive the special blessings God has prepared for us individually and experience the joy of living a Christian life as we serve and minister to all of humanity.

This book can be used as a guide for Christian pastors and teachers to utilize in helping their members and/or students to become acquainted with what is involved in determining our spiritual growth. It can be a vital source for pastors to determining the growth level of the congregation he serves. A Christian cannot grow spiritually with a measure of success when the believer has no clue as to what is involved in spiritual growth.

The apostle Paul said in I Corinthians, "When I was a child, I spake as a child, I understood as a child, I thought as a child: but when I became a man, I put away childish things." Note several truths taught in this passage.

First, no one comes into this world, be it the natural world or the spiritual world, already matured. All of us begin at the same place in our spiritual growth.

Secondly, all of us possess the power and potential for spiritual growth as Christians. There is no Christian that cannot grow spiritually. Christians are designed to grow and are expected to grow.

Thirdly, spiritual growth is not automatic. It requires of us to become a student of God's word, learning and practicing what we have learned. This cannot be accomplished apart from the direct involvement of the

Holy Spirit. He must govern and guide our learning and as we learn, He governs our opportunities to execute what we have learned. The Holy Spirit will guide us in accordance with God's timing to put to use that which we have learned in proportion to the need at hand. The more we learn and become obedient to the will of God, our spiritual growth will continue; and as we move to a different level, our ability to meet the challenges at that level provides the basis for further spiritual growth. Spiritual growth is not a product of what Paul says in II Timothy 3:7, "Ever learning, and never able to come to the knowledge of the truth." Spiritual growth is not supposed to be static, stunted, stationary, or infantile, it is supposed to be progressive, constantly moving, learning, and acquiring. All of which is to be governed and guided by the Holy Spirit.

Fourthly, proper appliance on the part of the Christian will assure us of spiritual growth. How much we give ourselves to Bible study, prayer, commitment to the will and works of God, and doctrinal learning, (What is meant by doctrinal learning is learning the principles, truths, values, and reasons for what the word of God says) will determine how strongly and firmly we grow spiritually. Spiritual growth, if not maintained, can result in stagnation and the loss of what progress we have attained. Paul speaks of this condition in Hebrews 5:12-13. He states, "For when for the time ye ought to be teachers, ye have need that one teach you again which be the first principles of the oracles of God; and are become such as have need of milk, and not of strong meat. For every one that useth milk is unskillful in the word of righteousness: for he is a babe." There is something about consistency that is essential to growing spiritually on a continuous basis.

Fifthly, spiritual growth is measurable. One of the keys in determining our spiritual growth is seen in how much of our childish behavior and conduct we have put away; we have overcome. If we are still behaving in the same childish ways as an adult as we did when we were children, we have not grown spiritually. There is a point in the Christian life where we have no appetite for undue criticism, engaging in slander, ridicule and gossip, envy, jealousy, and strife. If these things still have a grip on our lives, it is a sign of immaturity. We need to do this self-examination to see if we are yet childish in our conduct and behavior. If we are, we have not grown spiritually. It clearly is saying that we need to grow spiritually.

CONTENTS

INTRODUCTION 1

Chapter I 7

   TEXT: Gen. 1:3-5; John 3:3 7

   Day One/Level One 8

      Day One, "The New Birth" 8

   The Exposition 8

      God's Ability and Power to Recreate 9

      A New Beginning: The Journey of a Life Time 14

      The perfect work of God 16

   The Marks of Level One 17

   Applying the Marks of Level One 17

   Hindrances to Conquering This Level 20

   The Individual's Responsibility 21

Chapter II 22

   TEXT: Gen. 1:6-8; Col. 1:1-2 23

   Day Two/Level Two 24

      Day Two "Believers Being Separated from the World" 24

   The Exposition 24

      Extracted Truths and Principles from the Title 25

      Signs of Spiritual Immaturity 27

      Signs of Spiritual Maturity 28

- Growth Possibilities 28
- The Marks of Level Two 29
- Applying the Marks of Level Two 30
- Hindrances to Conquering This Level 33
- The Individual's Responsibility 34

Chapter III 36
- TEXT: Gen. 1:9-13; John 15: 2, 5,8 37
- Day Three/Level Three 39
  - Day Three, "Believers Bearing Fruit" 39
- The Exposition 39
- The Marks of Level Three 41
- Applying the Marks of Level Three 42
- Hindrances to Conquering This Level 46
- The Individual's Responsibility 47

Chapter IV 49
- TEXT: Gen. 1: 14-17; Acts 1:8 49
- Day Four/Level Four 51
  - Day Four, " Being A Witness and Testimony for Christ" 51
- The Exposition 51
- The Marks of Level Four 53
- Applying the Marks of Level Four 54
- Hindrances to Conquering This Level 58

Poor Witnessing / Testimony: A Direct Reflection of 59

The Individual's Responsibility 62

Chapter V 64

TEXT: Gen. 1: 20-23; I John 2:14-16 65

Day Five/Level Five 67

Day Five, "Believers Victorious Christian Life" 67

The Exposition 67

The Marks of Level Five 72

Applying the Marks of Level Five 73

Hindrances to Conquering This Level 77

The Individual's Responsibility 80

Chapter VI 81

TEXT: Gen. 1: 26-27; Rom. 8:28-29 81

Day Six/Level Six 83

Day Six, "Believers Service & Formation" 83

The Exposition 83

The Marks of Level Six 86

Applying the Marks of Level Six 88

Hindrances to Conquering This Level 95

The Individual's Responsibility 96

Chapter VII 98

TEXT: Gen. 2:1-3; Rev. 21:1 99

Day Seven/Level Seven 101

The Exposition 101
Bibliography 104
About the Author 105

ACKNOWLEDGEMENTS

There are some very special persons to whom I want to thank for their encouragement, urging, prodding, and supporting me to write this and other Bible based books.

To my wife, Jernice Ellis-Walls of whom I have been married for over fifty five years, thank you for being the encourager you are and praying that God would lead me to put what God has given me in print.

To our oldest daughter, Charnell Walls, thank you for your support and passion in urging me to take the leap and compile the mass amount of sermons, lectures, addresses and institute materials and share it with the world. Your willingness to take charge of the essential works to see that the drafts are critiqued and put in its final form was going beyond the call of duty.

To our second daughter, Hopi Walls, thank you for your encouragement and support in writing this book. Your review and help with so many of the details have kept me motivated to do the work necessary to writing when I felt like there was no time to do so.

To our third daughter, Trina Walls- Smith, your urging and encouragement over the years to write did not go unappreciated or unnoticed. You were always available to talk about the ministry and work God was doing through me. Thank you for all that you have done to make this book a reality.

To our fourth daughter, Cheryl Walls, thank you for your encouragement and questions that served as a source of motivation to write this book. Your critiquing skills have been most helpful in getting the content right.

Many thanks to all other Christian friends for your encouragement and support.

Without the approval of God, none of what this book offers would have ever been put in print, at least by me. Thank God for all of you

With Love,
Dr. Charles Walls, Th.D.

INTRODUCTION

Galatians 6:15, "For in Christ Jesus neither circumcision availeth anything, nor uncircumcision, but a new creature."

The beauty of this passage is that nothing is important in comparison to the work of God that occurs internally within the soul of man. The idea of a new creature is having a new birth. The record of recreation in Genesis 1:3-2:2, we have in shadow and type a picture of the spiritual creation, the new birth, and development of the believer for the purpose of revealing God's plan of redemption. Only Adam came into this world innocent. After Adam sinned, all after him came into this world with a sin nature. Something has to happen in order for our nature to become activated, which is, to commit our first sin. And something has to happen to activate our spiritual nature, which is, to be born again.

When God created the heaven and the earth as seen in Genesis 1:1, it was innocent, unmarred, and perfect (flawless). When Satan was kicked out of heaven and fell to earth, he disturbed it so that the earth became formless and void and plunged into invisibility, covered with water and shrouded in darkness. So it is with man, who comes into this world innocent, un-blemished, un-marred, and perfect for an un-interrupted life with God in peace, joy, and fulfillment. Man was made in the image and likeness of God.

The Devil, embodied in the serpent, interrupted the innocent and peaceful relationship man had with God. When Eve and Adam ate of the forbidden tree, it activated their carnal / sin nature. Thus, man now stood in need of saving. Where sin is, only the sacrifice of the Sinless One and the blood of the Atoning One, can provide proper covering for the sinner.

Genesis 1:2 says, "And the earth was (Heb. *hayah (haw-yaw* means became) without form (Heb. *tohaw (to-hoo)* means waste) and void; and darkness was upon the face of the deep." This is a Biblical picture of the results of the fall of man. When man sinned (All that came after Adam), he was not just wounded and therefore needed some doctoring up; he was not just sick and needed the medicine of culture, training, education, and determination to fix him up. Oh no! The sinner is dead, and broke with his God, and is lost, and helpless, and undone. The sinner without Christ is a total wreck. Nothing he can do has any merit with God.

The Bible is absolutely clear on this point. Notice Heb. 11:6, "Without faith it is impossible to please him (God)." Rom. 8:8, "They that are in the flesh cannot please God." Isa. 64:6, "All our righteousness is as filthy rags."

Man's attempt to make right his wrong by his own efforts will only amount to a patch and not a covering. Adam and Eve sewed fig leaves together for their covering, not knowing that what they needed was not about anything external, but rather internal, and that fig leaves left them exposed and unacceptable. They now needed transformation (internal changing that made them what was expected or required of them) and not conformation (external changing to look like what is expected or required).

The first creation though perfect (flawless) has now become waste, void, and in darkness is lifeless, hopeless, helpless, and lost, in its own right. There was nothing within the earth that could ignite a new beginning of itself. It contained nothing within itself that could begin a self-regeneration process. The disturbed earth would have remained lifeless, hopeless, helpless, and lost without outside intervention. No other personality or power could do anything about it outside of God, for the scripture declares, "And the Spirit of God moved upon the face of the waters (Gen. 1:2)." The picture here is that before man can experience the regeneration work of God, man has to renounce all claims of doing anything to help bring about his redemption. Our sins have rendered us utterly dead (lifeless, without any possible rejuvenation qualities or abilities in us), helpless, hopeless, and lost apart from Christ. It is only in this condition that God begins His work of making us a new creature.

When God begins the new creation process within us, how do we move from being saved to the next level of growth? Genesis teaches us what is required and how to identify where we are in comparison to the seven levels depicted by the six days of recreation and the seventh day of rest. Our growth is not about increasing activities, but rather, it is about increasing our Christian experiences and knowledge that expands our abilities to do ministry and live the Christian life. Increasing in activity is why the religious arena is ever growing in size / number without society getting any better.

We have majored in innovative ideas and have increased church activity and the masses are involved; yet life among the body has not shown signs of spiritual improvement. We can jump, shout, make noise, and all the other things and at the same time talk falsely about our brothers and sisters, refuse to give a helping hand to those among us with genuine needs, find fault without facts, compete with one another, and if we aren't careful, will cuss, take one another to unjust courts, and think it's okay. These characteristics are signs of our spiritual immaturity. We must remember that the Bible was written primarily for the purpose of revealing God's plan of redemption. This purpose is made possible and complete in the redemptive work of Jesus Christ as the Savior of the world. To understand the creation of the universe is to understand the new birth by which a sinner becomes a saint.

Every Christian is designed to grow in Christ. Growing spiritually is a life time journey. The apostle Paul says it best by the inspiration of God in Hebrews 6:1, "Therefore, leaving the principles of the doctrine of Christ, let us go onto perfection (Spiritual maturity); not laying again the foundation of repentance from dead works, and of faith toward God." We cannot go onto spiritual maturity without knowing what it means and what is involved.

The seven levels of spiritual growth are:

Day one / level one: "light" equals "new birth".

Day two / level two: "separation" equals "walk of believers, separated from the world".

Day three / level three: "creation of vegetation & fruit trees" equals "believers bearing fruit".

Day four / level four: "creation of light bearers" equals "believers witness and testimony".

Day five / level five: "creation of fish and fowl" equals "believers' victorious Christian life".

Day six / level six: "creation of cattle and man" equals "believers' service and formation into the image of Christ".

Day seven / level seven: "perfect peace and rest" equals "the ultimate goal of believers - our heavenly state with Christ".

Each one of these levels will be examined individually as outlined in the chapters. It is our responsibility to take this journey of understanding our spiritual growth which is a seven step journey. Each day of recreation and the seventh day of rest, when examined, will provide us with the requirements of each level of our spiritual growth.

Intentionally left blank.

Chapter I

Understanding Our Spiritual Growth
A Seven Step Journey to Spiritual Maturity:

Step One

We begin our spiritual journey with meeting the requirement of day one.

Day one equals our new birth. It is the place where each of us begins.

Let's get started.

TEXT: Gen. 1:3-5; John 3:3

Geneses 1:3-5, *"And God said, let there be light: and there was light. And God saw the light, that it was good: and God divided the light from the darkness. And God called the light Day, and the darkness he called Night, and the evening and the morning were the first day."* "

John 3:3, *"Verily, verily, I say unto thee, except a man be born again, he can not see the kingdom of God."*

Now let us begin looking at the teachings of creation to help us understand what is required in "Understanding Our Spiritual Growth: A Seven Step Journey: Step one.

Day One/Level One

Day One, "The New Birth"

The Bringing Forth of Light

Gen. 1:3, *"And God said, let there be light and there was light."*

John 3:3, *"Verily, verily, I say unto thee, except a man be born again, he cannot see the kingdom of God."*

The Exposition

In the interview between Nicodemus and Jesus, the question is, why was Nicodemus unable to understand what Jesus was teaching him about salvation? Answer. Nicodemus was lost, unsaved, dead, and blind to spirituality and before he could see spiritually, he had to have his spiritual sight given to him. This is step one, the first level in becoming a fully developed follower of Christ.

As the earth was created whole, good, perfect (flawless) and beautiful as Genesis 1:1 declares, so it was with man created upright and in the image and likeness of God. When Lucifer, now Satan, the devil, was expelled from heaven, he brought sin to earth.

His fall was so great that it disturbed the earth and the earth became formless and void and darkness was upon the face of the deep. As God began His recreation work in Genesis 1:2, "The spirit of God moved upon the face of the waters," so it is in our new birth, for scripture declares, "If any man be in Christ, he is a new creation," II Cor. 5:17.

As much as the earth could not overcome its dead, lifeless, hopeless, and helpless state after Satan's fall that caused it to be plunged into invisibility, messed up and wasted, no man can become saved by any works of his own. The Bible teaches that, "No man can come to me, except the Father which hath sent me draw him:" Jn. 6:44. Now let us note:

God's Ability and Power to Recreate

Gen. 1:3, "And God Said, let there be light: and there was light." In the original creation, God did not use any preexisting materials to create the heaven and the earth. When the Spirit of God begins His recreative work, He is working with existing materials.

> **A.** *The original creation* – Gen. 1:1, "In the beginning God created the heaven and the earth." In the original creation, God demonstrated His ability and power to bring forth something out of nothing. This is the essence in the meaning of the Hebrew word "bara". The earth was created whole, good, perfect (flawless) and beautiful as Genesis 1:1 declares. Likewise was man created upright and in the image and likeness of God as Gen. 1:26-27 declares.
>
> **B.** *The altered state of earth* – Gen 1:2, "And the earth was without form, and void; and

darkness was upon the face of the deep. And the Spirit of God moved upon the face of the waters." When Lucifer, now Satan fell and brought sin to earth, the earth became without form and void and darkness was upon the face of the deep. Likewise is it with man. When sin first entered man, man became altered from his original state. Man is filled with darkness, void of spiritual awareness and understanding. He has become messed up. As God began His recreation work in Genesis 1:2, "The spirit of God moved upon the face of the waters," so it is in our new birth, "if any man be in Christ, he is a new creation," II Cor. 5:17. It is the Spirit of God who convicts the sinful heart and causes it to respond positively to God's ability and power to recreate us and make us a new creature.

a. As much as the earth could not overcome its dead, lifeless, hopeless, and helpless state after Satan's fall that caused earth to be plunged into invisibility, messed up and wasted, no man can become saved by any works of his own. The Bible teaches that, "No man can come to me, except the Father which hath sent me draw him:" Jn. 6:44.

C. *God's ability and power are made known* – Gen. 1:3, "And God said, Let there be light:

and there was light." How does God make His ability and power known? God does it:

1. *By His words*, "And God said" God's words flow out of His will. What God wills, comes to pass. God has two separate wills. He has a direct will. In this will everything happens apart from the involvement of man. Note Jeremiah 1:5, "Before I formed thee in the belly I knew thee; and before thou camest forth out of the womb I sanctified thee, and I ordained thee a prophet unto the nations." God doesn't ask us if it is okay for it to rain, snow, storm, or be sunny. He does not ask us if it is okay for the sun to rise in the east or set in the west. He does not ask us if we want to be dark skinned or light skinned, male or female, short or tall. He does not ask us if stealing, adultery, backbiting, homosexuality, and the like are sins. God's direct will is always presented in His commands to us. There are no options in God's direct will. God also has a conditional will. The conditional will of God is determined by the options God

gives man. Words associated with God's conditional will are "if, when, as a result of, because, and then I". Note, if man repents, God will forgive. When man accepts the saving work of Jesus on Calvary, God will save him. God's ability and power are in His words.

2. *By His permission*, "Let there be" Nothing happens until God says so. Everything past, present, and future have been settled before time. Psalms 119:89 says, "For ever, O Lord, thy word is settled in heaven." God does not have to wait until something happens to make a decision. He settles all issues before hand and permits them to be acted out in time. When God says, "let there be", He is giving permission for His direct will to take form and actuality. Nothing happens in life or time that is not by God's permission. We may not understand what God is doing on any given situation, but we ought to rest in the fact that it is His will, direct or conditional, and it could not be without His permission. It is just another way

of God demonstrating His ability and power.

3. *With the products God produces -* "light" The Hebrew word for light is (*owr - ore*) - light, brightness, luminary, illumination, or enlightening. This is not the meaning of the Hebrew word used here. Light here is not the same as the luminaries in space, the sun, the greater light, the moon, the lesser light, or the stars. Here light is referring to "life". This word signifies life in contrast to death. It is the kind of life Jesus gives us at salvation, which is eternal life. The word for life is zoe, John 1:4. God' ability and power is not only demonstrated, seen and understood by His words and His permission, but thirdly, by what He produces. No one disputes others ability and power when tangible evidence is before us. Man measures ability and power by what we produce. The reason why we don't attach great titles to babies and the unskilled is because they have not produced anything that we can use as a model to justify such titles. Babies

and the unskilled are never called inventors, tycoons, masters, great artists, great minds, scholars, tremendous leaders, great chiefs, and etc. because they have not produced anything to justify such titles.

A New Beginning: The Journey of a Life Time

"Gen. 1:3B, "And there was light." This is where our spiritual journey begins. Light, meaning spiritual life, is the same as our new birth.

    D. *The miracle of life* - "And there was light (*owr – ore*). Here light is referring to "life". As previously stated, this word signifies life in contrast to death. It is the kind of life Jesus gives us at salvation, which is eternal life." This is the reason why the picture of day one speaks of the new birth. The new birth is the reception of spiritual light / life and constitutes the beginning of our spiritual journey toward spiritual maturity. We neither explain nor understand fully how God restructured the old into something new. The word that best describes His work is "miraculous". Who can explain with clarity and understanding how God took dust, dirt, mud, clay, soil, and turned it into flesh, blood, bone, brain, and it having mobility, speech, reasoning power and sensitivity? This can only be seen as and called miraculous. Our new birth is nothing short of a miracle. Every time a soul is conceived, it's a miracle; born, it's a miracle, and born again, it's a miracle.

E. *The symbol of spiritual life* - "light" It is by the "light" that our spiritual journey begins. This journey is about spiritual growth. If you cannot see, perceive, understand, or know that you have been born again, you need to right now, ask God to come into your life by repenting of your sin, confessing that you are lost and that you believe that Jesus is the only One who can save you. God will save you instantaneously. This is an imperative because you cannot do what is required of believers at the second level, day two, without meeting the requirement of level one, day one. The journey begins with being born again. If the new birth has not been experienced, the requirements of day two do not apply. Everything associated with spiritual growth must be done in a chronological order. You cannot do what is required on day two without meeting the requirements of day one.

The perfect work of God

Gen. 1:4, "And God saw the light, that it was good: and God divided the light from the darkness."

    A. *God's power of observation and perfect understanding* - "God saw" The Hebrew word (*raah, raw aw*) denotes God's omniscience – infinite knowledge and God's omnipotence – infinite power. God sees His work in the light of His perfection. The actuality of what God brings to bear genuinely exists, be it visible or invisible. God's ability to see is described in unusual terms: Proverbs 15:3, "The eyes of the Lord are in every place, beholding the evil and the good." II Chronicles 16:9, "For the eyes of the LORD run to and fro throughout the whole earth..." Proverbs 22:12, "The eyes of the LORD preserve knowledge..." Jesus is described in Revelations 1:14b, "and his eyes were as a flame of fire;" as One having eyes that are penetrating, seeing all things past, present, and future. Nothing is hid from His sight. He sees in the dark equally as well as in the light. It is by the "light, meaning spiritual life" that our spiritual journey begins. This journey is about our spiritual growth

The Marks of Level One

By marks we mean, the qualities or characteristics that identifies the makeup of any given level of growth. These are the characteristics that one must possess to be at the level specified. Level one marks are seen in manifesting:

> **A**. Spiritual Personality
> (Indwelling of the Holy Spirit)... Eph. 4:30
>
> **B**. Spiritual Sight... Jn. 9:25
>
> **C**. Spiritual Nature... Rom. 8:13-14
>
> **D**. Spiritual Appetite... I Cor. 2:11-15
>
> **E**. Spiritual Infancy... Heb. 5:13

Moving to the next level demands one to conquer the requirements of this level. Not to do so will result in one never getting started on their spiritual journey to become a fully developed follower of Christ and therefore it would be impossible to move to the next level.

Applying the Marks of Level One

Our Inspiration: Be ye therefore followers of God, as dear children – Eph. 5:1

How do we determine our spiritual growth at level one? If we are doing these works without dread, reservation, or the feeling of being forced, then we are conquering the requirements of this level. The works at this level are:

> *I. Demonstrate our Spiritual Personality (Indwelling of the Holy Spirit)...* Eph. 4:30, "Grieve not the holy Spirit of God, whereby ye are sealed unto the day of redemption." When does God afford us the opportunity to utilize our spiritual personality? He does it when we face the challenges of compliance with being obedient to the command seen in verses 31 and 32. These verses say, "Let all bitterness, and wrath, and anger, and clamour, and evil speaking, be put away from you, with all malice: and be ye kind one to another, tenderhearted, forgiving one another, even as God for Christ's sake hath forgiven you."
>
> **II**. *Manifest our spiritual sight...* Jn. 9:25, "He answered and said, Whether he be a sinner or no, I know not: one thing I know, that, whereas I was blind, now I see." Many times we may be confronted with the challenge to take a stand for Christ in opposition to great odds and personal safety. These are the times that tries our devotion to Christ. When God affords us the opportunity to speak in favor of Christ, we do so against the dangers involved. The devil wants the believer to deny Christ, but there is no denying of Christ when He converts us. The light we gain at the point of our salvation is too

powerful and too wonderful and too genuine to deny that we have been changed for the better.

III. *Live in our spiritual nature...* Rom. 8:13-14, "For if ye live after the flesh, ye shall die; but if ye through the Spirit do mortify the deeds of the body, ye shall live. For as many as are led by the Spirit of God, they are the sons of God." Daily we will be challenged to move out of our spiritual nature to comply with the works of the devil and the ways of the world. A life that is guarded and guided by the Spirit of God will always please God in all we do. Living in our spiritual nature makes us conquerors and overcomers. We will experience victories in our lives and will be able to encourage others of the benefits and blessings of living in our spiritual nature.

IV. *Maintain our spiritual appetite...* I Cor. 2:14-15, "But the natural man receiveth not the things of the Spirit of God: for they are foolishness unto them: neither can he know them, because they are spiritually discerned. But he that is spiritual judgeth all things, yet he himself is judged of no man." Our appetite determines our desire to eat or not eat. Spiritually, we have an appetite for the knowledge, ways, wisdom, and word of God. It is what keeps us seeking and pursuing spiritual understanding and spiritual wisdom. We want to know more of God and His ways, therefore we seek to participate in Bible studies and spiritual training. Where there is no spiritual appetite, there will not be any drive or passion for God and His word. We will refrain from encouraging others to participate in the same.

V. *Recognize that at this level, our spiritual growth is that of a spiritual infant...* Heb. 5:13, "For everyone that useth milk is unskilful in the word of righteousness: for he is a babe." We are just beginning our journey toward spiritual maturity. We are babes in Christ. Babes may not have the mind of a full grown man, but they have the potential of becoming one. Being a babe in Christ says that we have been born again and are ready to move to our next level of growth. When we learn these truths and apply them as God affords us the opportunity, we are understanding our spiritual growth: our seven step journey.

Hindrances to Conquering This Level

A. Our dead condition...Rom. 8:6-7

B. Our rejection of the Spirit's pricking of our hearts...Rom. 2:5

C. Our unwillingness to accept the Gospel message of salvation...John 3:36

D. Our denying of our need to be saved...John 12:48

E. Our blindness by Satan...II Cor. 11:3

F. Our love and comfortableness with darkness through the things of this world...John 3:19

The Individual's Responsibility

What is it that one has to do here in order to move to the next level, which is, "living a life of separation?" The steps here reveal and are gleaned from the teaching of Romans 10:1-14:

A. Hear the gospel...

B. Conviction by the gospel...

C. Confession...

D. Repentance...

E. Then cleansing...

If we have done these things, which constitute belief in Christ, then the blood of Jesus has washed our sin of unbelief away and we are saved. This is the beginning point of every saved person that makes us all equal in Christ because we all must start at the cross and proceed out from it on our discipleship journey.

Congratulations, you are now ready to move to the next level.

Intentionally left blank.

Chapter II

Understanding Our Spiritual Growth: A Seven Step Journey to Spiritual Maturity:

Step Two

In chapter I, we learned that the first day, first level of our spiritual growth represents our new birth. Once this level has been achieved, we are ready to move to the next level of our spiritual growth. Day two, level II represents our responsibility to separate ourselves from the world. Now let us continue the journey.

TEXT: Gen. 1:6-8; Col. 1:1-2

Genesis 1:6-8, *"And God said, let there be a firmament in the midst of the waters, and let it divide the waters from the waters. And God made the firmament, and divided the waters which were under the firmament from the waters which were above the firmament: and it was so. And God called the firmament Heaven. And the evening and the morning were the second day."*

Col. 3:1-2, *"If ye then be risen with Christ, seek those things which are above, where Christ sitteth on the right hand of God. Set your affection on things above, not on things on the earth."*

Now let us begin looking at day two of recreation to help us understand what is required in "Understanding Our Spiritual Growth: A Seven Step Journey: Level Two.

Day Two/Level Two

Day Two
"Believers Being Separated from the World"
The Firmament
Dividing the waters from the waters

Gen. 1:6, *"And God said, let there be a firmament in the midst of the waters, and let it divide the waters from the waters." Col. 3:1, "If ye then be risen with Christ, seek those things which are above, where Christ sitteth on the right hand of God."*

The Exposition

A recap of the first day

Day one / level one: "light" equals "New birth"

The Lord has given us seven levels of growth and what is involved at each level. These levels are presented to us symbolically in the recreation work of God over the seven days in Genesis 1:2-2:2.

From these seven levels, two objectives can be achieved: 1) to determine one's own level of spiritual growth by comparing the standards of each level with our understanding of our spiritual growth. 2) To learn the standards of each level and what is required for us to move from where we are to where we ought to be until all levels are completed.

The believer's greatest hindrance to winning others to Christ lies in the area of separation. The world is unimpressed by our saying "I'm a Christian" and we run with them and take part in their activities of sin. Scripture says and teaches in James 1:27, "Pure religion and undefiled before God and the Father is this, to visit the fatherless and widows in their affliction, and *to keep himself unspotted from the world*." This passage is teaching us how important it is to live a separated life. All Christians have spots but if our spots are to be known, let them be known among other believers and not the world.

Moving to the next level in our Christian growth demands living a separated life. As God separated the firmament from the waters and called it Heaven, Christians must realize that we are not designed to be interwoven with the world, but rather be separated from it. There must be a clear distinction between those who are believers and those in the world that are lost. We have given the requirements and teaching of day one/level one, the beginning of our spiritual growth. Now we are going to view the requirements of day two/level two of our spiritual growth.

Extracted Truths and Principles from the Title

When the title, "Understanding Our Spiritual Growth: A Seven Step Journey" is explored, it reveals some essential truths or principles.

First, the title is about sanctification. Sanctification is the process of being set apart for God's use. It is the believer's responsibility of doing all in this life to grow to spiritual maturity.

Secondly, there are thoughts, behaviors, and interactions that we must overcome in order to grow spiritually. We must overcome Selfishness - (Lk. 12:18-21), Envy - (Prov. 3:3, Rom. 1:29-31, I Tim. 6:4), Strife - (Phil. 2:3, I Tim. 6:4), and Vain Glory - (Phil. 2:3), just to name a few.

Thirdly, there are certain practices we must enhance in order to grow. It is not enough just to overcome the things that hinders us from growing spiritually, we must also take on the qualities that enhances our opportunity to grow spiritually. We must Build Christian relationships - (Prov. 18:24, Phil. 2:3-4) and Aide the needy - (II Tim. 2:15).

Fourthly, there are works we cannot afford to bypass because they are essential to spiritual growth. We cannot afford to bypass Prayer - (Acts 1:14, Phil 4:6-7, Col. 4:3), Bible Study - (II Tim. 3:15), Stewardship that cannot be negligent: Time - (Eph. 5:16, Col. 4:5), Talents - (I Cor. 12:31), and Treasures - (Matt. 25:14-30), and Worship - Isa. 1:11; Jer. 6:21. Worship occurs only when the heart of man joins with the heart of God for no other reason than adoration and communion. Worship is not what we do: To God - this becomes prayer or praise. .For God - this becomes ministry or service. .Because of God - this becomes thanksgiving or gratitude. Worship is what we do: With God - not as God's partner or servant, but "with", meaning, fused together, joined together, interwoven together with God.

Now let us note:

Signs of Spiritual Immaturity

A. *Immature conduct*...I Cor. 1:12-13A - "...I am of Paul, ...I am of Apollos, ...I am of Cephas, ...I am of Christ. Is Christ divided?"

B. *Doing only when things are as we desire*...Matt. 23:15 - "...For ye compass sea and land to make one proselyte"

C. *Doing if it is my idea*...II Tim. 4:3-4 - "...They heap to themselves teachers, having itching ears"

D. *Quitting when problems or troubles arise*...Heb. 6:6 - "If they shall fall away, to renew them again unto repentance;"

E. *Supporting those we like and playing favorites*... James 2:2-4 - "Are ye not then partial in yourselves,"

F. *Taking pleasure in the downfall of our brothers and sisters*...I Cor. 13:6 - "Rejoiceth not in iniquity,"

G. *Failing to render aide to the hurting*...Luke 10:31 - "...He passed by on the other side."

Signs of Spiritual Maturity

A. *Mature Discipleship*...Jn. 8:31 - "If ye continue in my word"

B. *Standing on the principles of God in the midst of life threatening situations or circumstances*...Rev. 2:8-11 - "...Be thou faithful unto death?

C. *Never giving up because the going gets tough*...James 1:12 - "Blessed is the man that endureth temptation:"

D. *Standing against all odds for right and righteousness*...Acts 7:54-60 - "...But he...looked up steadfast into *heaven,"*

E. *Always yielding to the guidance of God*...Matt. 26:42 - "...Thy will be done."

F. *Not allowing one's self to be controlled by our desires above the wishes of God*...Heb. 11:24-25 - "Moses...choosing rather to suffer affliction...than to enjoy the pleasures of sin for a season;"

G. *Always walking in the Spirit and not in the flesh*...Gal. 5:16 - "Walk in the Spirit, and ye shall not fulfil the lust of the flesh."

Growth Possibilities

A. It cannot ever happen without commitment to Christ - Jn. 6:64-69

B. It cannot happen without obedience to Christ - Jesus. 26:13

God separated the firmament from the waters and called it Heaven, Christians must realize that we are not designed to be interwoven with the world, but rather be separated from it.

There must be a clear distinction between those who are believers in Christ and those in the world. This distinction can be seen in the marks of level two.

Now let us note:

The Marks of Level Two

A. Loving Christ...John 14:21

B. Following the teachings of Christ...Rom. 16:17

C. Following after Divine knowledge and wisdom... Prov. 3:5-6

D. Choosing the right persons to partner with and build relationships...II Cor. 6:14- 16

E. Selecting the right place where we choose to grow...II Cor. 6:17

F. Rejecting Satan and his destructive schemes and offers...Col. 2:8

G. Shunning the appearance of evil...I Thes. 5:22

Most believers are stuck at level two in their Christian growth. The enticements and attractiveness of the things of the world do not appear to be bad or out of place to us. We think it is okay to mix the world's ways with those of God. The key statement we use at this stage is, "There is no harm in doing this or that." Making our first step is always the most difficult. We must comply with and conquer this level if there is any chance of us growing to perfection.

Applying the Marks of Level Two

Our Inspiration: "Be ye therefore followers of God, as dear children" – Eph. 5:1

Determining our spiritual growth at this level, they must also be done without dread, reservation, or the feeling of being forced. Our passion for the work of Christ keeps us doing the will of God freely. In doing these works willfully and willingly says we are conquering the requirements of this level. Here are the works we must do at this level.

> **I**. *We must show forth our love for Christ...* John 14:21, "He that hath my commandments, and keepeth them, he it is that loveth me: and he that loveth me shall be loved of my Father, and I will love him, and will manifest myself to him." In keeping the commandments of Christ, they will show up in the way we treat one another. We cannot love Christ without loving our fellow man. To obey Christ in the realm of

love is how we show forth our love for Christ. We do not put Christ behind anything, He is our priority and we follow Him.

II. *We must follow the teaching of Christ...* Romans 16:17, "Now I beseech you, brethren, mark them which cause divisions and offenses contrary to the doctrine which ye have learned; and avoid them." One of the demands of being a Christian is to follow the teachings of Christ. Our Christ life is to be carved out by the teachings of Christ. Jesus gave us many of His teachings in Matthew 5:14-48. Our Christian life is to reflect these and other teachings of Christ on a daily basis.

III. *We must follow after Divine knowledge and wisdom...*Proverbs: 3:5-6, "Trust in the Lord with all thine heart, and lean not unto thine own understanding. In all thy ways acknowledge him, and he shall direct thy paths." Pursuing knowledge and wisdom is an arduous task that spans over a life time. Solomon teaches us that we are to cry out after knowledge, and liftest up our voice for understanding; If thou seekest her as silver, and searchest for her as for hid treasures; Then shalt thou understand the fear of the Lord, and find the knowledge of God. For the Lord giveth wisdom: out of his mouth cometh knowledge and understanding. Prov. 2:3-6.

IV. *We must choose the right persons to partner with and build relationships...*II Cor. 6:14-16, "Be ye not unequally yoked together with unbelievers: for what fellowship hath righteousness with unrighteousness? And what communion hath light with darkness? And what concord hath Christ with Belial? Or what part hath he that believeth with an infidel?" Being in the right kind of relationship for Christians, builds strong ties and commitment to each other. The influence between Christians with Christians leads to greater understanding of Christ and greater loyalty to Christ and each other.

V. *We must reject Satan and his destructive schemes and offers...* Col.2:8, "Beware lest any man spoil you through philosophy and vain deceit, after the traditions of men, and not after Christ." We are warned of God to reject the destructive schemes and offers of the devil. To be caught up in the works of the devil will result in not being able to conquer the requirements of this level. We need the power of the Holy Spirit to enable us to reject the destructive schemes and offers of the devil. Without the enabling power of the Holy Spirit, the cunning ways Satan present his offers to us will seem right, rational, and rewarding, but the Holy Spirit sees through his plots and He shows us what Satan is doing.

VI. *We are admonished to shun the very appearance of evil...* I Thes. 5:22, "Abstain from all appearance of evil." When we face a situation that does not look right or feel right, the likelihood is it is not right. Again, we must lean heavily on the guidance of the Holy Spirit. He will not lead us into sin nor can He do so. Christians are given the power of discernment. It is designed to help us see what is right and wrong. What is right, we are to cling to, but what is wrong, we are to shun it.

Hindrances to Conquering This Level

Christians cannot afford to dress like the world, talk like the world, frequent the places and indulge in the practices of the world, pattern our religious services after the world, style our music like the world, acquire funds like the world, do business like the world, or build relationships like the world. The word of God warns us of these practices.

In II Corinthians 6:17, Paul addresses the Corinthian believers and admonishes them concerning idols by saying, "Wherefore come out from among them, and be ye separate, saith the Lord, and touch not that unclean thing;" The psalmist teaches us of the blessedness of being separated from the world. Note Psalms 1:1-3, "Blessed is the man that walketh not in the counsel of the ungodly, nor standeth in the way of sinners, nor sitteth in the seat of the scornful. But his delight is in the law of the LORD; and in his law doth he meditate day and night. And he shall be like a tree planted by the rivers of water, that bringeth forth his fruit in his season; his leaf also shall not wither; and whatsoever he doeth shall prosper."

The things that hinder believers at this level and keep us from moving to the next level are:

> A. Patterning ourselves by the world's standards...
>
> B. Doing what the world does with the world....
>
> C. Incorporating the works of the world with the works of God...
>
> D. Embracing the philosophy of the world as an acceptable and justifiable pattern for Christian life and growth...
>
> E. Trying to be all things to all people...
>
> F. Living life as though there are no absolutes...

Moving to the next level requires conquering this level of separation from the world. If you are not separated from the world, you cannot move to the next level, that of fruit bearing.

The Individual's Responsibility

What is it that one has to do here in order to move to the next level, which is, "fruit bearing?" The steps here are as follow, taught in Psalms 1:1-2 & Proverbs 3:5-7:

A. Refrain from carving your life out by the standards and teachings of the world - "Walketh not in the counsel of the ungodly"

B. Refrain from embracing or practicing the ways of the unsaved - "Nor standeth in the way of sinners"

C. Refrain from becoming satisfied with the childish and selfish behaviors of worldly power, prestige, and positions - "Nor sittest in the seat of the scornful"

D. Pursue the righteousness that is found only in God's word - Delight in the law of the Lord."

If we conquer this level of separation from the world, we can move to the next level, that of fruit bearing. Having done this, God elevates us to the next level and stipulates a new set of demands, commands, and requirements for us to continue in our spiritual growth. You are to be congratulated for compliance with the requirements of level two. Now you are ready to begin the journey to level three.

Intentionally left blank.

Chapter III

Understanding Our Spiritual Growth: A Seven Step Journey to Spiritual Maturity:

Step Three

In chapter II, we continued on the journey of Understanding Our Spiritual Growth: A Seven Step Journey. We learned that the first day, first level of our spiritual growth represented our new birth. The second day we learned that it represented our responsibility to separate ourselves from the world. Once level II has been achieved, we are ready to move to the next level of our spiritual growth. Day three, level III. It represents our responsibility to bear fruit, which is the work of evangelism. Now let us continue the journey.

TEXT: Gen. 1:9-13; John 15: 2, 5,8

Gen. 1:9-13, *"And God said, let the waters under the heavens be gathered together unto one place, and let the dry land appear: and it was so. And God called the dry land Earth: and the gathering together of the waters he called Seas: and God saw that it was good. And God said, let the earth bring forth grass, the herb yielding seed, and the fruit tree yielding fruit after his kind, where seed is in itself, upon the earth: and it was so. And the earth brought forth grass, and herb yielding seed after his kind, and the tree yielding fruit, whose seed was in itself, after his kind: and God saw that it was good. And the evening and the morning were the third day."*

John 15:2, 5,8, *"Every branch in me that beareth not fruit he taketh away; and every branch that beareth fruit, he purgeth it that it may bring forth more fruit (V2). I am the vine, ye are the branches, he that abideth in me, and I in him, the same bringeth forth much fruit (V5): here in is my father glorified that ye bear much fruit, so shall ye be my disciples (V8)."*

Now let us begin looking at day three of recreation to help us understand what is required in "Understanding Our Spiritual Growth: A Seven Step Journey." Step three.

Day Three/Level Three

Day Three, "Believers Bearing Fruit"

Creation of Vegetation and Fruit Trees

Gen. 1:11, "And God said, let the earth bring forth grass, the herb yielding seed, and the fruit tree yielding fruit after his kind, where seed is in itself, upon the earth: and it was so."

28 John 15:2, "Every branch in me that beareth not fruit he taketh away; and every branch that beareth fruit, he purgeth it that it may bring forth more fruit."

The Exposition

A recap of the first two days

>**A**. Day one / level one: "light" equals "New birth"

>**B**. Day two / level two: "separation" equals "Walk of believers, separated from the world"

In Genesis, God repeatedly uses the words, "after his kind". The grass produced grass (rye reproduced rye and not Bermuda); fruit trees reproduced fruit trees (apples brought forth apples and not bananas); etc. God built within each plant, animal, fowl, and human the power to reproduce after his kind.

Fruit bearing cannot be made any clearer than God has as He represents it on the third day of recreation. So then, what is the fruit of the believer? Don't confuse the "fruit of the Spirit" with that of the "fruit of the believer". The fruit of the Spirit is love, joy, peace, long suffering, gentleness, goodness, faith, meekness, and temperance (Gal. 5:22- 23). If we take the teaching from Genesis, "after his kind" then the fruit of the believer is another believer. So what does this mean? It means that the "fruit of the believer" is "soul winning". Soul winning is evangelizing. Matthew 28:19 says, "Go ye therefore and teach (Greek *matheteusate* means to make disciples or to win or lead another to Christ for salvation) all nations.

The fruit is like the tree. It is another tree in immaturity. Jesus said it this way in John 3:6, "That which is born of flesh is flesh and that which is born of spirit is spirit." Believers are to beget believers. Solomon understood this truth and put it this way, "The fruit of the righteous is a tree of life and he that winneth souls is wise (Prov. 11:30).

When we look at the teaching of John 15 on fruit bearing, three categories of fruit bearing are seen: 1) beareth fruit (V 2), 2) more fruit (V 2), and 3) more fruit (V 5,8). The figure given by Solomon says, the believer is a tree, and in that tree is the seed in each fruit for another potential tree, and in each tree there is fruit for the potential of more trees and as these trees bear fruit with seed, more potential trees may be produced.

The believer has not been made a tree to be barren or to practice birth control. Jesus said, "Make disciples of all nations". Don't be satisfied with leading only one person to Christ, or just your household, or your neighborhood. Have a passion for lost souls.

Notice Jesus' teaching about winning in John 15. When we lead one soul to Him, He will in turn increase our passion to lead others to Him, "Every branch that beareth fruit, he purgeth it, that it may bring forth more fruit (V 2)."

The ability to reproduce is not the work of the individual believer, but rather, it is the work of, "He who lives within us," the Holy Spirit. It is the Spirit who produces spiritual life in every soul.

The following are the characteristics we must execute at this level.

Now let us note:

The Marks of Level Three

A. Surrendering to the guidance of the Spirit...Jn. 16:13

B. Acquiring the knowledge of the word of God...Matt. 22:29

C. Having the knowledge of the plan of salvation...Acts 16:30-31

D. Be willing to share the gospel with the lost...Acts 26:20

E. Avoiding temptation to give up when the lost do not accept the gospel...Mark 5:5-6

F. Making sacrifices and bearing inconveniences in order to evangelize...Jn. 4:4

It is our responsibility to put forth every effort to develop the ability to comply with the requirements of this level. We are not alone in this effort, the Spirit is with us guiding and aiding us to obtain these Christian characteristics.

Applying the Marks of Level Three

Our Inspiration: "Blessed is the man that walketh not in the counsel of the ungodly, nor standeth in the way of sinners, nor sittest in the seat of the scornful" – Psa. 1:1

Our spiritual growth at this level shows up in these manners shown below. Each level of our spiritual growth adds to and expands our works in ministering to the needs of lost souls. If we are practicing these marks, we are on our way to conquering the requirements of this level. Again, we must do these works without dread, reservation, or the feeling of being forced.

I. *We must surrender to the guidance of the Spirit*... Jn. 16:13, "Howbeit when he, the Spirit of truth, is come, he will guide you into all truth: for he shall not speak of himself; but whatsoever he shall hear, that shall he speak:

and he will shew you things to come." To separate our selves from the world, we must walk in the Spirit of God. He will instruct us through the illumination of the word of God and direct us in accordance with that which is of God. It becomes our responsibility to surrender to the guidance of the Spirit. The Spirit will never guide us in any way that is contrary to the will of God and the way of Christ.

II. *We must acquire the knowledge of the word of God*...Matt. 22:29, "Jesus said unto them, Ye do err, not knowing the scriptures, nor the power of God." To be successful in the works of God, it is imperative for us to know the word of God. Knowledge of the word of God assures us of being accurate in our presentation when we speak regarding the truth of God. Without knowing the word of God, we will speak only that in which we know; that which is not in line with the word of God.

III. *We must have the knowledge of the plan of salvation*...Acts 16:30-31, "And brought them out, and said, Sirs, what must I do to be saved? And they said, Believe on the Lord Jesus Christ, and thou shalt be saved, and thy house." God will put people in our path that the Spirit has been moving on their heart to accept the gospel – the death, burial, and resurrection of Jesus Christ - that we have been given to share with them. We cannot share what we do not know.

To know the plan of salvation requires being taught the plan of salvation. We cannot afford to wait until we are faced with an opportunity to share God's plan of salvation to try and present it to the lost, it must be known beforehand if we are going to have any measure of success in presenting it.

IV. *We must be willing to share the gospel with the lost...*Acts 26:20, "But shewed first unto them of Damascus, and at Jerusalem, and throughout all the coast of Judaea, and then to the Gentiles, that they should repent and turn to God, and do works meet for repentance." The unsaved needs the gospel to be saved. It is required of believers to learn the plan of salvation and then be willing to take it to the unsaved and share it with them. To have a passion for lost souls makes us willing to share the gospel to the lost. All areas will be our spheres of operation in sharing the gospel to the lost. Our willingness to share the gospel will afford us the opportunities to share in all areas.

V. *We must avoid the temptation to give up when the lost do not accept the gospel...*Mark 5:5-6, "And he could there do no mighty work, save that he laid his hands upon a few sick folk, and healed them. And he marveled because of their unbelief. And he went round about the villages, teaching."

The work of evangelism is so important for any of us to give up when the lost do not accept God's appeal through the gospel to be saved. Jesus marveled at the unbelief of those in His home town, but it did not stop Him from continuing to share the good news. Where one may not accept or a thousand may not yield one convert, still, there are others out there waiting to hear the gospel and accept it. It is worth having a thousand to reject when the thousand and one accepts.

VI. *We must make sacrifices and bear inconveniences in order to evangelize...* Jn. 4:4, "And he must needs go through Samaria." Jesus said in Luke 14:23, "And the Lord said unto the servant, go out into the highways and hedges, and compel them to come in, that my house may be filled." This work of God assigned to believers will bring us face to face with many hurdles to cross. The primitive conditions of the lost and the places of the lost can be most challenging. God requires of us to make great sacrifices and endure many inconveniences to get the gospel to those that are lost. I have worked in both the domestic and foreign fields and many sacrifices and inconveniences were brought to bear. But the joy of leading a lost soul to Christ drives out the stress associated with sacrificing and the burdens of inconveniences.

Hindrances to Conquering This Level

What hinders us from winning souls? Fear is the main cause. Fear says, I'm not able, it's too dangerous, the time is not right, they ought to come to church and get saved, that is for the preacher or others to do, and/or that is not my calling, etc.

The Seed (the Holy Spirit) is in us, so we are able. We go into areas far more dangerous when we go all over towns and cities interviewing and talking to people we don't know about jobs, products, etc., so soul winning is not too dangerous for us to do. Is there a better time to cast a lifeline to a drowning man than when he is struggling to keep from drowning? No! The lost are drowning and need the lifeline of Christ, which is the gospel, cast to them. The time to cast the lifeline is now, for the field is ready for harvest. Jesus sent us out to win and not to stay home and draw, so we need to go. We are trees and not just the preacher, so it's every believer's ministry to do, every tree has been equipped with fruit producing ability from our spiritual birth, thus it is part of every believer's assignment. To be a tree is to develop to that symbolic state through proper teaching and training.

Things that hinder us from conquering this level and moving to the next are:

    A. Fearing failure, rejection, and physical harm...

B. Fearing incompetency as a result of inexperience...

C. Not allowing the Spirit to guide us...

D. Lacking proper training and skill levels...

E. Hiding out amongst other ministries to keep ourselves from being exposed to a soul winning opportunity...

F. Accepting false concepts that say soul winning is another's responsibility...

Moving to the next level requires conquering this level of fruit bearing. Not to conquer it keeps us from moving to the next level, that of being a true witness and testimony for Christ.

The Individual's Responsibility

What is it that one has to do here in order to move to the next level, which is, "witnessing and testimony?" The steps here are as follow, derived from John 15:1-8:

A. Remain in the vine - walk in the Spirit of God...

B. Be planted in the right place - find your area of ministry...

C. Be exposed to sunlight - power resulting from studying, meditating, and heeding the written word...

D. Draw from the soil: water and nutrients - partnering with faithful, refreshing, encouraging, and loving believers...

E. Inward conversion of digestible intake - obediently yielding to the power of the Lordship of Christ who works through our Christian character and shows up outwardly in the blossoms that produce fruit...

F. Not resist the care of the caretaker - to heed the leadership of the man of God whose ministry it is to watch for your souls (by weeding your field, cultivating your soil, and fertilizing your tender plant)...

Everyone who is successful in complying with the requirements of this level, God blesses even more than the past two levels. Every level conquered lifts us higher and higher, thus, we are expanded in our capacity to do more and be blessed more. If you have complied here, congratulations, you are ready to move to level four.

Chapter IV

Understanding Our Spiritual Growth: A Seven Step Journey to Spiritual Maturity:

Step Four

In chapter III, we continued on the journey of Understanding Our Spiritual Growth: A Seven Step Journey. We learned that the first day, first level of our spiritual growth represented our new birth. The second day we learned that it represented our responsibility to separate ourselves from the world. The third day we learned that it represents our responsibility to bear fruit, which is the work of evangelism. Once level III has been achieved, we are ready to move to the next level of our spiritual growth. Day four, level IV. It represents our responsibility to be a witness and testimony for Christ. Now let us continue on our journey.

TEXT: Gen. 1: 14-17; Acts 1:8

Gen. 1: 14-17, *"And God said, let there be lights in the firmament of the heaven to divide the day from the night...and let them be for lights in the firmament of the heaven to give light upon the earth: and it was so. And God made two great lights; the greater light to rule the day, and the lesser light to rule the night: he made the stars also. And God set them in the firmament of the heaven to give light upon the earth."*

Acts 1:8, *"But ye shall receive power, after that the Holy Ghost is come upon you: and ye shall be my witnesses unto me both in Jerusalem, and in Samaria, and unto the uttermost part of the earth."*

Now let us begin looking at day four of recreation to help us understand what is required in "Understanding Our Spiritual Growth: A Seven Step Journey." Step four.

Day Four/Level Four

Day Four, "Being A Witness and Testimony for Christ"

Being light bearers,
Reflecting the light of Christ

Gen. 1: 14-17, "And God said, let there be lights in the firmament of the heaven to divide the day from the night...and let them be for lights in the firmament of the heaven to give light upon the earth: and it was so.

Acts 1:8, "But ye shall receive power, after that the Holy Ghost is come upon you: and ye shall be my witnesses unto me both in Jerusalem, and in Samaria, and unto the uttermost part of the earth."

The Exposition

A recap of the first three days

    A. Day one / level one: "light" equals "New birth"

    B. Day two / level two: "separation" equals "Walk of believers, separated from the world"

    C. Day three / level three: "creation of vegetation & fruit trees" equals "Believers bearing fruit"

When fruit bearing (soul winning) is mastered, our passion for winning souls makes us prime for witnessing and being a living testimony for Christ.

Genesis fourth day speaks of "light bearing" that is the same for believers. It equals our being a witness and testimony for Christ. Genesis also says He made the stars also. The greater light (the sun) represents God the Father, the lesser light (the moon) represents His son on earth, and the stars represent believers. Daniel writes in Daniel 12:3, "They that be wise shall shine as the brightness of the firmament: and they that turn many to righteousness, as the stars for ever and ever."

Jesus is no longer present in the flesh here on earth. One day Jesus will return to earth to reign, He will come as the Sun of Righteousness. He will flood the earth with His glory. In His ascension, His absence from earth now, constitutes the night, a period of darkness. What is the source of light for the night? It is the moon and stars. In this dark world, Jesus has not left this period without a source of light. The Church is His moon reflector reflecting the light of the Sun of Righteousness and believers are His star reflectors as individuals to shed forth His light. Jesus said in Matthew 5:14-16, "Ye are the light of the world. A city that is set on a hill cannot be hid. Neither do men light a candle, and put it under a bushel, but on a candlestick; and it giveth light to all that are in the house. Let your light so shine before men that they may see your good works, and glorify your Father which is in heaven."

Notice Genesis statement about the stars, "God set them in the firmament of the heaven to give light upon the earth (V 17)." "Set in heaven" is where every believer is in Christ.

God sees us, the believers in Christ, as though we are already seated with Christ in heaven. Eph. 2:5-6 state it this way, "...quickened us together with Christ...and hath raised us up together, and made us sit together in heavenly places in Christ Jesus:" This is our present position in Christ as God looks upon every believer.

The following are the characteristics we must possess at this level.

Now let us note:

The Marks of Level Four

A. Availability to Christ... I Cor. 11:1

B. Commitment to Christ... Matt. 16:24

C. Demonstration of the life of Christ lived in and through us...Gal. 2:20

D. A willingness to share Christ wherever we are...Matt. 28:19,

E. To take a stand for the principles and teachings of Christ even when facing overwhelming odds... Acts 26:22-23

F. Place the ministries, works, and services of God above those of society, institutions, organizations, others, and self...Jn. 21:15-17

Moving to the next level requires conquering this level of witnessing and testimony. The higher God elevates us, the more difficult the task becomes to comply with

God's standards. More things get in the way, but be encouraged, as you have made it to this point, God will get you through this one as He has in the past levels.

Applying the Marks of Level Four

Our Inspiration: "But if ye walk in the light, as he is in the light, we have fellowship one with another, and the blood of Jesus Christ his Son cleanseth us from all sin." – I John 1:7

We have made it successfully through three levels of our spiritual growth. We are to be congratulated for what we have achieved thus far. We are at level four of our spiritual growth in which we are to be a witness and testimony for Christ. If we are practicing these marks, we are on our way to conquering the requirements of this level. Again, we must do these works without dread, reservation, or the feeling of being forced.

> **I**. *We must make ourselves available to Christ...* I Cor. 11:1, "Be ye followers of me, even as I also am of Christ." Christ is our model, our example, and our guide. When we minister to others, we must do so in the same manner as Christ. Charles Sheldon, in his book, In His Steps, stated repeatedly, (and I paraphrase) in every situation we face, our course of action is what would Jesus do in this situation? We should never take a course of action that Jesus would not take.

II. *We must commit ourselves to Christ...* Matt. 16:24, "Then said Jesus unto his disciples, If any man will come after me, let him deny himself, and take up his cross, and follow me." Commitment is not starting and stopping, being in one day and out the next, or claiming to be with Christ and not doing what He says. Commitment is denying self and clinging to Christ in every possible way. It is obeying Christ's commands at the time he commands them. Commitment is twenty four hours a day, three hundred and sixty five or six days a year. It is following Christ when it is easy and when it is hard.

III. *We are to model the life of Christ lived in and through us...* Gal. 2:20, "I am crucified with Christ: nevertheless I live, yet not I, but Christ liveth in me: and the life which I now live in the flesh I live by the faith of the Son of God, who loved me, and gave himself for me." The life we live must reflect the life of Christ living in and through us. When others see us, they ought to see the life of Christ in us. The best witness and testimony we can be is when our lives reflect the life of Christ. Christ loved His enemies as well as His friends. He met the need of man and obeyed the will of His Father. Christ never attempted to do anything before clearing His actions with the Father. We too are to be the same kind of witness and testimony for Christ as Christ was for the Father.

IV. *We must be willing to share Christ wherever we are...*Matt. 28:19, "Go ye therefore, and teach all nations, baptizing them in the name of the Father, and of the Son, and of the Holy Ghost:" Jesus has commanded us to go and teach all nations. The word teach means in the original language, as we are going, make disciples. Wherever we are, we are expected to share Christ to others. This mandate of Christ leaves no one out, all are included. Wherever we are, we are to share Christ.

V. *We are to take a stand for the principles and teachings of Christ even when facing overwhelming odds...* Acts 26:22-23, "Having therefore obtained help of God, I continued unto this day, witnessing both to small and great, saying none other things than those which the prophets and Moses did say should come:

That Christ should suffer, and that he should be the first that should rise from the dead, and should shew light unto the people, and to the Gentiles." The story of Paul before the officials of Rome teaches us that we, like Paul, must take a stand on the principles and teachings of Christ even when facing overwhelming odds. The risk we face in being a witness for Christ is often overwhelming. The effect of taking such a stand may result in many being led to Christ for salvation.

VI. *We are to place the ministries, works, and services of God above those of society, institutions, organizations, others, and self*...Jn. 21:15-17, "So when they had dined, Jesus saith to Simon Peter, Simon, son of Jonas, lovest thou me more than these? He said unto him, Yea, Lord; thou knowest that I love thee. He saith unto him, Feed my lambs. He saith to him again the second time, Simon, son of Jonas, lovest thou me? He saith unto him, Yea, Lord; thou knowest that I love thee. He said unto him, Feed my sheep. He saith unto him the third time, Simon, son of Jonas, lovest thou me? Peter was grieved because he said unto him the third time, Lovest thou me? And he said unto him, Lord thou knowest all things; thou knowest that I love thee. Jesus said unto him, Feed my sheep." Is there anyone or anything we love more than Christ? If so, we will not conquer the requirement of this level until we do. A true witness and testimony for Christ comes when we make Christ first in our lives. We cannot afford to let parents, brothers, sisters, relatives, friends, enemies, jobs money position, prestige, or power take the place of Christ in our lives.

Hindrances to Conquering This Level

While stars were placed in heaven, they were to shine upon earth. Christians are stars set in the heaven, but shining on earth. As stars shining on earth, we are left here to shine among men. This old world is roaming around in darkness looking for a way out and that way is only found in Jesus Christ. It becomes the responsibility of the stars to shed the light of Christ with those who are stumbling in the dark. When Jesus was here, He said, "as long as I am in the world, I am the light of the world" (John 9:5). He is no longer here, but before He left, He committed the light to believers. Jesus said, "Ye are the light of the world. A city that is set on a hill cannot be hid...let your light so shine before men, that they may see your good works, and glorify the Father which is in heaven (Matt. 5:14,16)."

Everywhere believers go we are to share the gospel with lost souls. We are to be Christ's witnesses and testimony.

In Matthew 28:18-20, note these words or phrases, "All power, all nations, whatsoever I have commanded you, and I am with you". These words or phrases give us, "The four all" of the great commission.

They are respectively, all power - our provisions; all nations - our responsibility; all His word: whatsoever I have commanded you - our authority; I am with you - our assurance and sufficiency, all His Presence: To put it another way, His command is our commission, His word is our message and power, the world is our arena, and He (Jesus) is our source and sufficiency. Because of this, we have no reason not to be His witness and testimony. As much as stars are hidden behind other stars and no light is reflected from them, and as much as the eclipse of the sun hinders the moon and stars from receiving and reflecting light, so are there obstacles, hindrances, and other objects that hinder, halt, and keep believers from being Christ's witness and testimony.

Poor Witnessing / Testimony: A Direct Reflection of

I. *Being in the wrong places for the wrong reasons*. Stars that are in the enemy's territory often are there to keep from being the witness God desires - as Abraham was in Egypt. God told him to remain in Canaan. Abraham viewed life from his eyes (the eyes of man) and not from God's eyes. To Abraham, Egypt had a better plan than that of God. Egypt's plan looked more profitable and prosperous and God's plan, to Abraham, was one of famine and hardship... Gen. 12:10-20

II. *Excuse making* - When God calls us to follow Jesus, too many believers resort to excuse making as those exposed in Luke 14:15-27. There are those who make family the excuse for not being a witness and living testimony for Christ. Others use work as being the excuse for not being so. Others use domestic ties as an excuse for not witnessing and testifying for our Savior.

III. *Lack of spiritual / Biblical knowledge* - How foolish the thought that we do not have to prepare ourselves to do God's will. Bible classes are offered and most stay away. The most non-participant, infrequent, less attended area of ministry of the Church is Christian education (Bible study). Ignorance is an absorber and not a reflector. Matt. 22:23-29, an account of an occasion where a group came to Jesus asking whose wife will a woman be in heaven who married two brothers on earth. Jesus replied, "Ye do err not knowing the scriptures, nor the power of God..." Light and truth are woven together and cannot be separated. There is no such thing as light and untruth, light and falseness, light and sin. These are incompatible. They never merge. Thus, there is no witnessing and testimony for Christ where there is no knowledge of Him, or when error is present.

IV. *Improper Associations* - Proverbs 29:3 states, "Whosoever loveth wisdom rejoiceth his father: but he that keepeth company with harlots spendeth his substance." Proverbs 29:9 says, "If a wise man contendeth with a foolish man, whether he rage or laugh, there is no rest." These passages warn us of the consequences of associations (the company we keep). Who believers make their running buddy has a direct bearing on their ability to reflect the light of Christ. Wrong company usually brings about wrong actions and behaviors. The principle is not one of affiliation, but rather, one of participation. Notice Solomon's words are "keepeth company with harlots, and contendeth with a foolish man," both speak of participation that results in no good outcome.

V. *Destructive Preoccupations* - Believers walking in what pleases them materialistically, socially, economically, personally. To be locked in to the works that do not reflect Christ is detrimental to being a strong and positive witness and testimony for Christ. Destructive preoccupations reflect the ways of the world and not Christ.

VI. *Our lack of true Christian experiences* – It is common place that too many testimonies have nothing to do with Christianity. What we experience in the world is often stated as being a Christian experience. Christian experience are experiences that the world cannot claim. When we claim that we won a prize and claim it was a blessing from God, the world says I was on a TV game show and won cash, a car, and a trip to a special resort in a foreign country. How is this different? If we testify that the Lord gave me peace in the midst of a crisis, the world cannot make the same claim.

To summarize the hindrances to this level. They are:

    A. Being in the wrong places for the wrong reasons

    B. Excuse making

    C. Our lack of spiritual/ Biblical knowledge

    D. Improper associations

    E. Destructive preoccupations

    F. Our lack of true Christian experiences

Moving to the next level requires conquering this level of being a witness and testimony for Christ. If we do not master day four, we cannot get to the next level, day five. God wants us to be a witness and testimony wherever we are and go. Be so, on the job, in the home, in the community, at school, during vacation, business trips, times of tragedy, wartime, peacetime, and all times by just redeeming the times!

The Individual's Responsibility

What is it that one has to do here in order to move to the next level, which is, the "Believers Victorious Christian life?" The steps here are:

    A. Pray... Lk. 11:1-4

    B. Evangelize... Mk. 16:20

    C. Forgive... Matt. 18:21-22; Lk. 17:4

    D. Show mercy... Rom. 12:10

E. Express love to the undeserving... Matt. 5:44

F. Exemplify exhortation...Acts 20:2

G. Live a godly life...I Tim. 2:2-3

H. Give your testimony...Amos 3:13

I. Embrace the works of God that fall outside of your gifts and talents...I Thes. 5:14

J. Preach if possible...Rom. 10:15

K. Help make it possible for others to preach...II Cor. 11:9

L. Support Christian mission...Rom. 15:26

M. Love humanity...I Thes. 4:9

If we have conquered the demands of day four, again, congratulations, your growth is proceeding well and God is saying to you as He did with the days of recreation, "It is good". You are ready to move to level five.

Intentionally left blank.

Chapter V

Understanding Our Spiritual Growth:
A Seven Step Journey to Spiritual Maturity:

Step Five

In chapter IV, we continued on the journey of Understanding Our Spiritual Growth: A Seven Step Journey. We learned that the first day, first level of our spiritual growth represented our new birth. The second day we learned that it represented our responsibility to separate ourselves from the world. The third day we learned that it represented our responsibility to bear fruit. The fourth day we learned that it represented our responsibility to be a witness and testimony for Christ. Once level IV has been achieved, we are ready to move to the next level of our spiritual growth. Day five, level V. It represents our responsibility to live a victorious Christian life. Now let us continue on our journey.

TEXT: Gen. 1: 20-23; I John 2:14-16

Gen. 1:20-23, *"And God said, let the waters bring forth abundantly the moving creatures that hath life, and fowl that may fly above the earth in the open firmament of heaven. And God created great whales, and every living creature that moveth...and God blessed them, saying, be fruitful and multiply, and fill the waters and the seas, and let fowl multiply in the earth... the fifth day."*

I John 2:14-16, *"...I have written unto you, young men, because ye are strong, and the word of God abideth in you, and ye have overcome the wicked one. Love not the world, neither the things that are in the world. If any man love the world, the love of the Father is not in him. For all that is in the world, the lust of the flesh, and the lust of the eyes, and the pride of life, is not of the Father, but of the world."*

Now let us begin looking at day five of recreation to help us understand what is required in "Understanding Our Spiritual Growth: A Seven Step Journey." Step five.

Day Five/Level Five

Day Five, "Believers Victorious Christian Life"

Defying the Pull of This World:

Gen. 1:20-23, "And God said, let the waters bring forth abundantly the moving creatures that hath life, and fowl that may fly above the earth in the open firmament of heaven.

I John 2:14, "...I have written unto you, young men, because ye are strong, and the word of God abideth in you, and ye have overcome the wicked one." I John 5:4-5, "For whosoever is born of God overcometh the world, and this is the victory that overcometh the world, even our faith. Who is he that overcometh the world, but he that believeth that Jesus is the Son of God?"

The Exposition

A recap of the first four days

>**A.** Day one / level one: "light" equals "New birth"
>
>**B.** Day two / level two: "separation" equals "Walk of believers, separated from the world"
>
>**C.** Day three / level three: "creation of vegetation & fruit trees" equals "Believers bearing fruit"

D. Day four / level four: "creation of light bearers" equals "Believers witness and testimony"

The fifth day God created fish and fowl. These animals fill the waters and the sky. In order for fish to swim and dive to great depths without damage or destruction, they have to defy or overcome the tons of pressure exerted upon them from the water. The forces of nature have to be defied or overcome. When fishes sink to great depths, they adjust their air bladder and cell pressure to balance the pressure of the water.

Birds have to overcome the pull of the earth by a very unique method. These animals are able to allow another force, an unseen force, to lift them above the gravitational pull of the earth and soar high into the heavens. This unseen force is air. All the bird has to do is open up or spread its wings and permit the wind (air in motion) to get under its wings and the wind carries the bird up and away in the heavens above the earth. A bird never really flies, it just leans on the wind and the wind lifts the bird out of the grips of gravity that pulls and tugs and strives at keeping it on the ground. When there is no wind, birds flop their wings to create wind that they can lean on to be lifted to heavenly heights. Without wind, there will be no soaring.

Both the Old and New Testaments denote Wind and Spirit with the same Hebrew word, *raucil* and Greek word, *pneuma*. Like fowls of the air have to rely on another force to defy gravity, believers must rely on the

Spirit of God to produce the power to overcome the pull of this world. Note a few passages: Gal 5:16, "This I say then, walk in the Spirit, and ye shall not fulfill the lust of the flesh." One of man's greatest struggles is that of the flesh. It is more than a notion to cause our fleshly desires to be brought under subjection. Paul cries out in utter misery as he struggles with the problem of bringing his flesh under control. Listen to what he says in Rom. 7:24-25, "O wretched man that I am! Who shall deliver me from the body of this death? I thank God through Jesus Christ our Lord." What a struggle we all have and the answer is found in Christ who gave us the Spirit to empower us to bring our struggle into subjection.

Note again Paul's statement in I Cor. 9:27, "But I keep under my body, and bring it into subjection: lest that by any means, when I have preached to others, I myself should be a castaway." We are able to have victory over this struggle, not by removing the temptation or the desire, but by spreading our wings of faith and allowing the Wind / the Holy Spirit to lift us above this earthly, fleshly pull. Here is how the Apostle teaches us to fly. Note, Rom. 6:12-13, "Let not sin therefore reign in your mortal body, that ye should obey it in the lust thereof. Neither yield ye your members as instruments of unrighteousness unto sin: *but yield yourselves unto God,* as those that are alive from the dead, and your members as instruments of righteousness unto God."

When our struggles seem to get the best of us, let us recall the words of the Psalmist in Ps. 35:4-5, 7,

"*Delight* thyself also in the LORD; and he shall give thee the desires of thine heart. *Commit* thy way unto the LORD; *trust* also in him; and he shall bring it to pass. *Rest* in the LORD, and *wait* patiently for him: fret not thyself because of him..." Paul furthers these instructions in Phil. 4:6-7, "*Be careful for nothing*; but in everything by prayer and supplication with thanksgiving let your request be made known unto God. And the peace of God, which passeth all understanding, shall keep your hearts and minds through Jesus Christ."

If there is any one truth in all these passages, it is, there is victory for the believer to live the Christian life in this dark, sinful, and gravitational world. A world that is out to keep us bound to earth. But God has made us so we can soar to heavenly heights in thinking, in behavior, in speech, in fellowship, in giving, in praising, in laboring, in relationships, in family ties, in good works, in moral standings, in ethical practices, and in common sense matters. We do not have to go through life defeated. We have the Wind / The Holy Spirit to lean on and He will make us conquerors and victors.

We just have to remember the words of I Jn. 4:4, "Ye are of God, little children, and have overcome them: because greater is he that is in you, than he that is in the world." We are victors because He, the Spirit, the Wind has made us so. What is the gravitational pull of the world that believers must overcome? These gravitational pulls fall in three categories that are the following: (I Jn. 2:16)

> **A**. *The lust of the flesh* - These are our carnal passions, things the flesh craves, physical pleasures, such as sensuality - partying, pornography, homosexuality, seduction, drugs, alcohol, prostitution, etc.
>
> **B**. *The lust of the eyes* - These are things mentally, physically or aesthetically pleasurable such as, new toys, clothing, houses, vehicles, philosophical views, transactional meditation, etc. This includes envy/covet – begrudging and desiring what belongs to another with the intent of getting it and leaving them without.
>
> **C**. *The pride of life* - The word pride is translated "boasting or vainglory". The idea in this word "pride" is pretentious ostentation that results from not seeing the emptiness of the things of the world. (Pretentious - arrogance, haughty - better than attitude; ostentation - profession / sating / declaring) The word "life" *bios,* not *zoe. Zoe* refers to the vital principle of life, while *bios* refers to life's possessions. Thus "the pride of life" is a boastful and arrogant attitude in the possession of worldly goods.

What are the characteristics we must possess and conquer at this level before we will be able to take on the works of level six? These are the characteristics we are to possess at this level. Now let us note:

The Marks of Level Five

A. Living in compliance with and under the guidance of the Holy Spirit... Rom. 8:1

B. Being prayerful in all things daily... Lk. 18:1

C. Knowing and following the teachings of the word of God...Matt. 22:16

D. Frequently spending time in worship with the Lord...Heb. 10:25

E. Partnering with God in doing good works... I Cor. 3:9

F. Utilizing the full armor of God in battling Satan and his forces...Eph. 6:11

G. Resisting the Devil... Ja. 4:7

H. Never rejecting the strength of other believers who are walking in the same paths we are... Eph. 5:15 & 21

To move to the next level, we must conquer these requirements. Satan is going to put everything he can in our path to keep us from doing so. We have the power and assurances of God that we can be more than conquerors through Christ who strengthens us.

Applying the Marks of Level Five

Our Inspiration: "Ye are of God, little children, and have overcome them: because greater is he that is in you, than he that is in the world" – I John 4:4

God has brought us through four of the seven steps in Understanding Our Spiritual Growth: A Seven Step Journey. We have learned how to conquer the requirements of day one – being born again, day two – separating ourselves from the world, day three – bearing fruit, day four – being a witness and testimony for Christ, and now day five, we will learn how to live the victorious Christian life. This level, like the previous levels, can only be conquered without dread, reservation, or the feeling of being forced.

> **I.** *We must live in compliance with and under the guidance of the Holy Spirit...* Rom. 8:1, "There is therefore now no condemnation to them which are in Christ Jesus, who walk not after the flesh, but after the Spirit." Living the victorious Christian life is a journey of faith of daily decisions that constitute our lifestyle that reflects Christ. We cannot live the victorious Christian life without the Holy Spirit governing and guiding us. This walk is a walk of faith. Daily we must decide to yield ourselves to the guidance of the Holy Spirit. As the apostle Paul said, "I die daily," I Cor. 15:31. We are admonished to crucify the passions of the flesh so we can live in the Spirit. Today's decision

will not suffice for tomorrow. It is a daily decision and faith walk.

II. *We must be faithful in prayer in all things daily*...Lk. 18:1, "And he spake a parable unto them to this end, that men ought to always pray, and not to faint;" A healthy prayer life is most essential to living the victorious Christian life. In everything we are to pray and pray consistently. Prayer is designed to help us line up with the will of God and not for God to line up with our will. A good habit in prayer is to pray to start our day, pray during the course of the day, pray for having been brought through the day, and pray for safety to see the next day. This was the practice of Jesus and we ought to follow His lead.

III. *We must know and follow the teachings of the word of God*...Matt. 22:16, "And they sent out unto him their disciples with the Herodians, saying, Master, we know that thou art true, and teachest the way of God in truth, neither carest thou for any man: for thou regardest not the person of men." Unscrupulous men will attempt to derail us from living the victorious Christian life. When we have come to know the truth, we can live in the truth. There are so many false teachers and preachers among the ranks of Christendom and we must be discerning to know them. Our victory lies in knowing God's word and following its teaching on a daily basis.

IV. *We must frequently spend time in worship with the Lord*...Heb. 10:25, "Not forsakening the assembling ourselves together, as the manner of some is; but exhorting one another: and so much the more, as ye see the day approaching." Worship is personal and individualized. Even when we meet at the house of God together, worship is between the individual and God. Worship occurs when the believer's heart connects with the heart of God and the two commune together. It is through true worship that our Christian life is lived victorious and we are transformed by the power of God alone. Warren Weirsbe says in his book, Real Worship, that worship involves wonder. We must spend time with God in worship to experience the wonder of it all.

V. *We must partner with God in doing good works*... I Cor. 3:9, "For we are labourers together with God: ye are God's husbandry, ye are God's building." God has chosen to have us participate in the works He is doing. The works of God are good works. To partner with God is to join God in doing what God is doing. It is a privilege and an honor to participate in the good works of God. Doing good works, not only helps others, they help us when we do them. Doing good works have a way of connecting us with God who in turn blesses us beyond measure.

VI. *We must utilize the full armor of God in battling Satan and his forces...* Eph. 6:11, "Put on the whole amour of God, that ye may be able to stand against the wiles of the devil." We are in a spiritual battle against the devil every day. He wants to conquer us, defeat us, and make us subject to him and not God. For our protection, God dresses us with the right armour for the battle. Our armour is the shield of faith, the helmet of salvation, the sword of the Spirit, and prayer. God equips us with the right armour for battle and He is with us during the battle.

VII. *We must be vigilant in resisting the Devil...* Ja. 4:7, "Submit yourselves therefore to God. Resist the devil, and he will flee from thee." First we must submit ourselves to God before we can resist the devil. God enables us and empowers us to resist the devil.

This is not simply saying to the devil, "Be gone," and the devil will flee from us. Jesus warned His disciples about false confidence in thinking that they had the power to put the devil to flight. Jesus said, do not boast about your simple success, for the day will come when you will say to the devil, Be gone, or to the sick. Be healed, and the devil will not move and the sickness will not go away. Resisting is to be done in the Lord, for it is He that gives us the power to say no to the offers of the devil.

VIII. *We must never reject the strength of other believers who are walking in the same paths we are...* Eph. 5:15 & 21, "See then that ye walk circumspectly, not as fools, but as wise. Submitting yourselves one to another in the fear of God." When we partner and fellowship with other believers, we can lean and draw on their strength to aide us in maintaining our victorious Christian life.

Hindrances to Conquering This Level

The natural pull of gravity is an un-relentless force against soaring. None of us, on our own, have the power within us to overcome gravity's pull. Man is no match for sin. We have weak and blind spots and Satan knows exactly what they are and where they are. Satan does not often attack our strengths, he uses our weaknesses to neutralize or make our strengths ineffective. Example: One may ever be so strong in loving his fellow man, but have problems in telling the truth or being dependable. The lack of truth telling and dependability will override one's love because others will not believe we are real and therefore, they will not allow us the opportunity to be trusted in other areas of our dealings with them. If we have trouble telling the truth, we can rest assured that Satan will create a situation where we will do nothing but prevaricate or falsify.

Throughout time Satan has used man's weaknesses to trap him, confuse him, embarrass him, dethrone him, ruin him, and destroy him. Here are a few historical proofs of Satan's untruthful dealings:

> A. Eve's desire to be over Adam. Satan used it so Eve could usurp Adam's authority... Gen. 3:1-6
>
> B. Cain's jealousy. Satan used it and caused Cain to kill his brother Abel... Gen. 4:8
>
> C. Sampson's immaturity and love of playing games. Satan used it and caused Sampson to lose his strength...Jud. 16
>
> D. David's love of beautiful women, Satan used it and caused David to commit adultery and murder...II Sam. 11:2-4
>
> E. Solomon's thirst for pleasure. Satan used it and caused him to have seven hundred wives, princesses, three hundred concubines...I Ki. 11:3
>
> F. Ananias and Sapphire's love of recognition and money. Satan used it and caused them to hide, scheme, and be untruthful...Acts 5:1-5 G. Our thirst and greed for power, position, and prestige. Satan uses it to entice us into committing sin...John 2:15-17

Satan is a master at manipulation. He is the world's greatest non-Christian psychologist. He has not the power to make us do anything or the ability to read our minds. But, he has the ability to observe our responses to certain stimuli and it's through this means that Satan influences and makes his appealing offers to us. What are some of the hindrances to living a victorious Christian life? They are:

    A. Walking in self...

    B. Walking in pride...

    C. Walking in a haughty spirit...

    D. Being controlled by greed...

    E. Being overcome with envy...

    F. Allowing jealousy to rule us...

    G. Being controlled by prejudices...

    H. Having a competitive spirit...

    I. Seeking after the big three "P"s - power, prestige, position

    J. Dishonesty in our dealings with others...

    K. Lack of faith in God and His word...

Moving to the next level requires us conquering the requirements of level five, living the believer's victorious Christian life. We will not get to the next level, that of service and formation, until we do.

The Individual's Responsibility

What is it that one has to do here in order to move to the next level, which is, "service and formation in the image of Christ?" It is our responsibility, figuratively speaking, to spread our wings and soar. The steps here are as follow:

>**A**. Love not the world or the things of the world... I Jn. 2:15
>
>**B**. Yield unto God... Rom. 6:13
>
>**C**. Delight in God... Ps. 40:8
>
>**D**. Commit to God... III Jn. 11
>
>**E**. Trust in God... Ps. 18:30
>
>**F**. Pray about everything... I Thes. 5:17-18
>
>**G**. Rest in God and all He is, does, and promises... Ps. 37:7a
>
>**H**. Wait patiently for God to act... Ps. 37:7b
>
>**I**. Lean on the Spirit and His power to lift us... Ja. 4:10

Having met the requirements of this level, you are ready to move to the next level, level six.

Congratulations for having complied with the requirements and demands of this challenging level.

Chapter VI

Understanding Our Spiritual Growth: A Seven Step Journey to Spiritual Maturity:

Step Six

In chapter VI, we continued on our journey of Understanding Our Spiritual Growth: A Seven Step Journey. We learned that the first day, first level of our spiritual growth represented our new birth. The second day we learned that it represented our responsibility to separate ourselves from the world. The third day we learned that it represented our responsibility to bear fruit. The fourth day we learned that it represented our responsibility to be a witness and testimony for Christ. The fifth day we learned that it represented our responsibility to live a victorious Christian life. Once level V has been achieved, we are ready to move to the next level of our spiritual growth, Day Six, Level VI. It represents the believers' service and formation into the image of Christ. Now let us continue on our journey.

TEXT: Gen. 1: 26-27; Rom. 8:28-29

Gen. 1:26-27, *"And God said, let us make man in our image, after our likeness: and let them have dominion over the fish of the sea, and over the fowl of the air, and over cattle, and over all the earth, and over every creeping thing that creepeth upon the earth. So God created man in his own image, in the image of God created he him; male and female created he them."*

Rom. 8:28-29, *"And we know that all things work together for good to them that love God, to them who are the called according to his purpose. For whom he did foreknow, he also did predestinate to be conformed to the image of his Son, that he might be the firstborn among many brethren."*

Now let us begin looking at day six of recreation to help us understand what is required in "Understanding Our Spiritual Growth: A Seven Step Journey." Step six.

Day Six/Level Six

Day Six, "Believers Service & Formation"

Made in the Image and Likeness of God

Gen. 1:26, "And God said, let us make man in our image, after our likeness: and let them have dominion over the fish of the sea, and over the fowl of the air, and over cattle, and over all the earth, and over every creeping thing that creepeth upon the earth."

Rom. 8:28, "And we know that all things work together for good to them that love God, to them who are the called according to his purpose."

The Exposition

A recap of the first five days

A. Day one / level one: "light" equals "New birth"

B. Day two / level two: "separation" equals "Walk of believers, separated from the world"

C. Day three / level three: "creation of vegetation & fruit trees" equals "Believers bearing fruit"

D. Day four / level four: "creation of light bearers" equals "Believers witness and testimony"

E. Day five / level five: "creation of fish and fowl" equals "Believers live a victorious Christian life"

The progress of the days of recreation, beginning with "let there be light" and it culminates in the image of God. This is the ultimate goal God had in mind from the beginning. It is God's goal and purpose for which He saves every believer. It is not only God's intent to save us from the lake that burns with fire and brimstone, but God's goal, aim, and purpose is to make us ultimately in His very image. The image of God is Jesus Christ. This truth is spoken of by the apostle Paul in Hebrews 1:1-3, "God, who at sundry times and in divers manners spake in time past unto the fathers by the prophets, Hath in these last days spoken unto us by his Son, whom he hath appointed heir of all things, by whom also he made the worlds; Who being the brightness of his glory, and the expressed image of his person..."

Jesus Christ is the expressed image of God the Father, and God's ultimate purpose for those saved is to make us like Jesus.

From the beginning when God said let there be light, He had in mind the crowning act of creation, which is the making of a man in the image of God. When God chose to save man, He had in mind the culmination of salvation, which is the perfect image of God, better expressed is to make us like His Son Jesus Christ.

From the beginning of our salvation, everything moves toward that goal expressed in that majestic, inexhaustible, unfathomable passage of Romans 8:28-29 that say, "And we know that all thing work together for good to them that love God, to them who are the called according to his purpose. For whom he did foreknow, he also did predestinate to be conformed to the image of his Son, that he might be the firstborn among many brethren."

The truth of verses 28-29 leaves no doubt that we are ultimately designed to be in the image of Jesus Christ. But in addition, what a wealth of truth there is in verse 30 which says, "Moreover whom he did predestinate, them he also called: and whom he called, them he also justified: and whom he justified, them he also glorified." The bottom line teaching is that God does it all for us from start to finish. There should not be any doubt as to how we will become like Christ. God will accomplish it and we can rest in knowing this tremendous truth.

Is there anything we are to do in regards to becoming like Christ? Absolutely. We are to serve as God assigns us ministry opportunities. Yet it is not our service that makes us like Christ. Our service comes after we have risen to the levels of our spiritual growth. This is the reason why we can determine exactly where each one of us is in our spiritual growth. The service we are able to do as ascribed in each level becomes our measuring rod. Wherever we are in our spiritual growth says exactly how much we are like Christ.

When we conform to the image of God, no longer do we act like men without any God, acting on our own accord. The more we conform to the image of Christ, we rid ourselves of:

A. All manners of abuse...

B. Muggings...

C. Murdering...

D. Slandering...

E. Childishness...

F. And the like...

Now let us note:

The Marks of Level Six

A A disciplined life... Job 36:10

B. Facing reality with confidence (not shadow boxing)... Dan. 3:16-18

C. Able to properly handle doctrines (eating meat)... Heb. 5:12-14

D. Not controlled by the things of this world (money, materialism, etc.)... Acts 4:36-5:3

E. Living in obedience to God's word and will... Acts 5:29

F. Having perfected spiritual abilities... Eph. 4:12-13

G. Having learned and know what spiritual gift(s) God has given us... I Cor. 12:7-11, 31

H. Walk in accord with the prompting of the Holy Spirit... Gal. 5:16 J. Delight in well doing...Gal. 6:9

I. We will be exhorters... Rom. 12:8

J. Delight in well doing...Gal. 6:9

K. Redeem the time by recognizing and taking advantage of every opportunity to do good... Eph. 5:16-17

L. We are second mile Christians... Matt. 5:41

M. We refrain from under-minded, underhanded, devious behavior in dealing with others who use such methods in dealing with us... II Cor. 13:7

N. We pray for our enemies as well as our friends and family... Lk. 6:28

O. We live in love and peace, as much as it is possible, with all men... Rom. 12:18

The characteristics of service and formation are where every believer ought to set his / her sights. It is truly the mark of our high calling of God in Christ Jesus. When or if we have to face death as many of the martyrs before us did, we too can say like Paul, "I'm now ready" or as the Hebrew children, "we will not bow".

Applying the Marks of Level Six

Our Inspiration: "For whom he did foreknow, he also did predestinate to be conformed to the image of his Son, that he might be the firstborn among many brethren." – Rom. 8:29

God has brought us through five of the seven steps in Understanding Our Spiritual Growth: A Seven Step Journey to Spiritual Maturity. We have learned how to conquer the requirements of day one – being born again, day two – separating ourselves from the world, day three – bearing fruit, day four – being a witness and testimony for Christ, day five - live the victorious Christian life. Now day six – believer's service and formation, in this level, like the previous levels, can only be conquered without dread, reservation, or the feeling of being forced.

> **I**. *We must display a disciplined life...* Job 36:10, "He openeth also their ear to discipline, and commandeth that they return from iniquity." Christians are to live a disciplined life. We are to refrain from living like the people of the world one day and like children of God the next day. Our lives are under control and it reflects the life of Christ in us. An undisciplined life is a life out of control and one that does not reflect the life of Christ in us. This life is not a dependable life.

II. *We must face reality with confidence (not shadow boxing)...* Dan. 3:16-18, "Shadrach, Meshack, and Abednego, answered and said to the king, O Nebuchadnezzar, we are not careful to answer thee in this matter. If it be so, our God whom we serve is able to deliver us from the burning fiery furnace, and he will deliver us out of thine hand, O king. But if not, be it known unto thee, O king, that we will not serve thy gods, nor worship the golden image which thou hast set up." Shadow boxing is boxing against an imaginary opponent. Dealing with idols is not imaginary, it is real. We have a real opponent, the devil, and he does not fight fair. Therefore we need to face him in the power of the Lord. Confidently, we must make sure our relationship with the Lord is intact. The Lord will fight our giants for us and give us victory.

III. *We must prepare ourselves so that we are able to properly handle doctrines (eating meat)...* Heb. 5:12-14, "For when for the time ye ought to be teachers, ye have need that one teach you again which be the first principles of the oracles of God; and are become such as have need of milk, and not strong meat. For everyone that useth milk is unskillful in the word of righteousness: for he is a babe. But strong meat belonging to them that are of full age, even those who by reason of use have their senses exercised to discern both good and evil."

Getting to know the teaching of God, we must sit at the feet of God's prepared servant that has the knowledge of Biblical truth. We cannot get to know what is needed without the assistance of God's prepared teacher. To properly handle the teaching of God is not the same as learning it. To handle doctrine is to share it accurately when we teach it.

IV. *We must not allow ourselves to be controlled by the things of this world (money, materialism, etc.)...* Acts 4:36-5:3, "And Joses...having land, sold it, and brought the money, and laid it at the apostles' feet. But a certain man named Ananias, with Sapphira his wife, sold a possession. And kept back part of the price, his wife also being privy to it, and brought a certain part, and laid it at the apostles' feet. But Peter said, Ananias, why hath Satan filled thine heart to lie to the Holy Ghost, and to keep back part of the price of the land?" Greed is a terrible sin. It plots and schemes to gain possession of more goods and material things, preferably money. This monster is one that we must constantly fight to overcome. The love of money is the root of all evil. The things of the world are pulling at us, desiring to control us. Christians have access to the power to deny these lures of the world.

V. *We must live in obedience to God's word and will...* Acts 5:29, "Then Peter and the other apostles answered and said, We ought to obey God rather than men." The benefits and blessings associated with obeying the word and will of God is beyond imagination. It is our assurance that we will be blessed of God. God requires of all His followers to live in obedience to His word and will.

VI. *We must perfect our spiritual abilities...* Eph. 4:12-13, "For the perfecting of the saints, for the work of the ministry, for the edifying of the body of Christ: till we all come in the unity of the faith, and of the knowledge of the Son of God, unto a perfect man, unto the measure of the stature of the fullness of Christ." Perfecting our spiritual abilities is for the purpose of ministering to others effectively. The church is the beneficiary of our perfected abilities. We are to minister to others until we all come into the fullness of Christ.

VII. *We must learn and know what spiritual gift(s) God has given us...* I Cor. 12:8 - 11,31, "...For to one is given by the Spirit the word of wisdom; to another the word of knowledge by the same Spirit; To another faith...the gift of healing...workers of miracles... prophecy... discerning of spirits... divers kinds of tongues... interpretation of tongues. But all these worketh that one and selfsame Spirit, dividing to every man severally as he will. But covet earnestly the best gifts: and yet shew I unto you a more excellent way." We need to get to know what spiritual gift(s) the Holy Spirit has given us. These gifts will determine our area of ministry.

VIII. *We must walk in accord with the prompting of the Holy Spirit...* Gal. 5:16, "This I say then, Walk in the Spirit, and ye shall not fulfill the lust of the flesh." The Spirit is not forcing. We must choose to yield to His guidance. The Spirit's prompting is always to lead us in the ways of righteousness and to do good works.

IX. *We must delight in well doing... Gal. 6:9,* "And let us not be weary in well doing: for in due season we shall reap, if we faint not." The life of the believer is to reflect the works of God. There may be some who may not appreciate the good we do for them. Our responsibility is to do good and leave the way others receive it up to them and God. There will always be someone we can do good unto. When doing good delights us, we will continue doing good.

X. *We must put forth as much effort in redeeming the time by recognizing and taking advantage of every opportunity to do good...* Eph. 5:16-17, "Redeeming the time, because the days are evil. Wherefore be ye not unwise, but understanding what the will of the Lord is." To do good is to redeem the time. We are to make the best use of the opportunities God affords us. We must refrain from engaging in the works of evil. Evil is all around us and it wants us to join in with its works. We must rely and lean on God for strength to endure in these evil days. Where sin did abound, the grace of God much more abound. Walking in the Spirit, obeying the word and will of God, and yielding to the leadership of the Holy Spirit will lead us in redeeming the time.

XI. *We must understand that Christians are expected to be second mile Christians...* Matt. 5:41, "And whosoever shall compel thee to go a mile, go with him twain." Second mile Christians are Christians who display a different attitude than that of the world. We are conquerors when we go the second mile. We are to show the world that Christians are different and we do the unexpected.

XII. *We must maintain the kind of prayer life that blesses our enemies as well as our friends and family...* Lk. 5:44, "Bless them that curse you, and pray for them which despitefully use you, and persecute you:" Jesus commands us to pray for our enemies, love our enemies, and do the same for friends and family. Praying for one's enemy is to wish him well and that his life would change for the better.

XIII. *We must live in love and peace, as much as it is possible, with all men...* Rom. 12:18, "If it be possible, as much as lieth in you, live peaceably with all men." This requirement comes with some room for failure. There are times we may not be able to live peaceably with some people. It may come on our part and the part of the other person. As much as it is in me to live peaceably with others is saying that we may have some short comings when it comes to living peaceably with all men. Yet we are commanded to do so to the best of our ability.

XIV. *We must refrain from under-minded, underhanded, devious behavior in dealing with others who use such methods in dealing with us...* II Cor. 13:7, "Now I pray to God that ye do no evil; not that we should appear approved, but that ye should do that which is honest, though we be as reprobates

Christians are not to allow ourselves be brought down to the level of wrong doers. When evil is done to us, our path is to do good to them. We are to overcome evil with good.

XV. *We must strive daily to be exhorters...* Rom. 12:8, "Or he that exhorteth, on exhortation: " An exhorter is one who comes along side of another and encourages. This is not to say that we do not point out the sin in others, but in spite of their sins, the exhorter encourages and supports others to move beyond their sin. Anyone can point out the sins of others, but to help others when they sin is a far greater work than being critical.

Hindrances to Conquering This Level

A. Walking in self...

B. Half-hearted commitment...

C. Partial obedience...

D. Following the paths of least resistance...

E. Becoming stagnated in our growth...

F. Becoming complacent with the status quo...

G. Being revengeful...

H. Setting up unforgivable parameters...

I. Allowing the will of God to be viewed from the flesh instead of from His Spirit...

J. Desiring those things that are not of God...

To move to the next level as a fully developed follower of Christ, we must conquer the requirements of this level. We cannot be moved to Level seven without conquering any of the levels after level one. The new birth will get us into heaven. Our spiritual growth will determine the size of our capacity to experience the blessings and joys of heaven. It is to our advantage to grow spiritually so that we can be the recipients of the fullness God has in store for all who gets there.

The Individual's Responsibility

What is it that one has to do here in order to move to the next level, which is, perfect peace and rest.

A. Commit totally to the will of God... Ps. 37:5, Prov. 3:5-7

B. Lean on the guidance of the Holy Spirit... Gal. 5:16

C. Delight ourselves in the word of God... Ps. 1:2

D. Remain rooted and grounded in the doctrines of God... Prov. 4:2

E. Do good to all men especially unto them who are of the household of faith... Gal. 6:10

F. Develop an active prayer life for all, especially for our enemies... Matt. 5:44

G. Leave vengeance up to God in all matters... Rom. 12:19

H. Exemplify mercy to the highest degree... Rom. 12:8D

I. Demonstrate genuine love even in extreme cases... Acts 7:59-60

J. Labor with joy even when it is our greatest challenge to do so alone... Rom. 8:35

If we are yet in the process of conquering the divine demands herein set, we have no time for finger pointing, criticizing, belittling, or any other derogatory behavior. All of our time ought to be spent doing what it takes to become fully matured.

If we have conquered, are serving, and are conformed to the image of Christ, we know what joy it is to be a mature Believer. Congratulations are in order and to all, a well-deserved promotion to the next level of perfect peace and rest.

Intentionally left blank.

Chapter VII

Understanding Our Spiritual Growth: A Seven Step Journey to Spiritual Maturity:

Step Seven

In chapter VI, we continued on our journey of Understanding Our Spiritual Growth: A Seven Step Journey. We learned that the first day, first level of our spiritual growth represented our new birth. The second day we learned that it represented our responsibility to separate ourselves from the world. The third day we learned that it represented our responsibility to bear fruit. The fourth day we learned that it represented our responsibility to be a witness and testimony for Christ. The fifth day we learned that it represented our responsibility to live a victorious Christian life. The sixth day we learned that it represented the believer's service & formation. Once level VI has been achieved, we are ready to move to the next level of our spiritual growth, Day Seven, Level VII. It represents the believers' perfect peace and rest. It equals the ultimate goal of believers - our heavenly state with Christ.

TEXT: Gen. 2:1-3; Rev. 21:1

Gen. 2:1-3, *"Thus the heavens and earth were finished, and all the host of them. And on the seventh day God ended his work that he had made, and he rested on the seventh day from all his work which he had made. And*

God blessed the seventh day, and sanctified it; because that in it he had rested from all his work which God created and made."

Rev. 21:1, *"And I saw a new heaven and a new earth, for the first heaven and the first earth were passed away; and there was no more sea." Now let us look at day seven in "Understanding Our Spiritual Growth: A Seven Step Journey." Step seven*

Day Seven/Level Seven

Gen. 2:1, - "Thus the heavens and earth were finished, and all the host of them." Rev. 22:4, "And they all shall see his face; and his name shall be in their foreheads."

The Exposition

A recap of the first six days

> **A**. Day one / level one: "light" equals "New birth"
>
> **B**. Day two / level two: "separation" equals "Walk of believers, separated from the world"
>
> **C**. Day three / level three: "creation of vegetation & fruit trees" equals "Believers bearing fruit"
>
> **D**. Day four / level four: "creation of light bearers" equals "Believers witness and testimony"
>
> **E**. Day five / level five: "creation of fish and fowl" equals "Believers live a victorious Christian life"
>
> **F**. Day six / level six: "creation of cattle and man" equals "believers' service and formation into the image of Christ"

Not many Christians will get to experience the six steps of our spiritual growth. Those of us who are blessed to live long enough and grow to and conquer each stage of our spiritual growth will have a greater capacity for experiencing joy in heaven. This is the level we are to strive to achieve. Heaven is waiting for all of us that have given our lives to Christ for salvation.

The question is, what level of spiritual maturity will we be when the Lord summons us home to be with Him?

Some will only experience day one of our spiritual growth before they are summoned home to be with the Lord.

Some will experience day two of our spiritual growth before they are summoned home to be with the Lord.

Some will experience day three of our spiritual growth before they are summoned home to be with the Lord.

Some will experience day four of our spiritual growth before they are summoned home to be with the Lord.

Some will experience day five of our spiritual growth before they are summoned home to be with the Lord.

Some will experience day six of our spiritual growth before we are summoned home to be with the Lord.

We pray that the mass of the remaining Christians living today will make it through day six before we are summoned home to be with the Lord in peace and rest.

Intentionally left blank

Bibliography

Real Worship by Warren Wiersbe

In His Steps by Charles Sheldon

The Wycliffe Bible Commentary edited by Charles F. Pfeiffer and Everett F. Harrison

Elemental Theology by Bancroft

The Analytical Greek Lexicon Revised 1978 Edition by Harold K. Moulton

Studies in Hebrews by Herschel H. Hobbs

The Hebrew - Greek Key Study Bible, KJV by Spiros Zodhiates

Our Daily Bread by Richard De Haan

The Holy Spirit by Charles C. Ryrie

Witnessing Without Fear by Bill Bright

Church Administration Hand Book by Bruce B. Powers

Spiritual Gifts by Smith Wigglesworth

A Ministering Church by Gaines S. Dobbins

The Spiritual Man by Watchman Nee

The Journey to Spiritual Maturity by Jamie Buckingham

Experiencing God by Henry T. Blackaby & Claude V. King

About the Author

**Dr. Charles Walls, Th. D –
Dean, Faculty, Finance\
B. Th., Th. M., Th. D**

**International Theological Seminary
217 S Warren St,
Lufkin, TX 75901
(936) 639-3011**

info@itsyourschool.org

Religious Preparation
Conroe College
Conroe, Texas

International Bible Institute & Seminary
Orlando, Florida

Academic Preparation
University of Wisconsin
Madison, Wisconsin

University of Houston Down Town
Houston, Texas

Durham College
Houston, Texas

U.S. Army School of Engineering
Ft. Belvoir, Virginia

U. S. Army Communication School
Augusta, Georgia

Angelina College
Lufkin, Texas

Areas of Concentration – Civil and Mechanical Engineering and Communications

Vocational Participation
President of Supporting People of Our Neighborhood Organization (SPOON)
Diboll, Texas

Dean of Texas State Missionary Baptist Congress
Port Arthur, Texas

Dean of East Texas #2 District Congress
Nacogdoches, Texas

Director of Academics, Central Christian University
Wynne, Arkansas

Board Member, Central Christian University
Wynne, Arkansas

Post Adjutant. Post 938, American Legion
Lufkin, Texas

National Baptist Convention, U.S.A. Inc.
Nashville, Tennessee

Church Affiliation
Pastor of Greater New Zion Baptist Church
Jacksonville, Texas

www.ingramcontent.com/pod-product-compliance
Lightning Source LLC
Chambersburg PA
CBHW062115080426
42734CB00012B/2873